POLEPOLE

POLEPOLE

A TRAINING GUIDE FOR
KILIMANJARO
AND OTHER LONG-DISTANCE MOUNTAIN TREKS

Angela deJong and Erinne Sevigny Adachi

RMB

Text copyright © 2019 by Angela deJong and Erinne Sevigny Adachi

Fitness photography copyright © 2019 by Claudine Lavoie

First Edition

For information on purchasing bulk quantities of this book, or to obtain media excerpts or invite the author to speak at an event, please visit rmbooks.com and select the "Contact" tab.

RMB | Rocky Mountain Books Ltd.
rmbooks.com
@rmbooks
facebook.com/rmbooks

Cataloguing data available from Library and Archives Canada
ISBN 9781771603133 (paperback)
ISBN 9781771603140 (electronic)

Cover photo: Above the clouds on Kilimanjaro
© iStock.com/ munro1

Printed and bound in China

We would like to also take this opportunity to acknowledge the traditional territories upon which we live and work. In Calgary, Alberta, we acknowledge the Niitsitapi (Blackfoot) and the people of the Treaty 7 region in Southern Alberta, which includes the Siksika, the Piikuni, the Kainai, the Tsuut'ina and the Stoney Nakoda First Nations, including Chiniki, Bearpaw, and Wesley First Nations. The City of Calgary is also home to Métis Nation of Alberta, Region III. In Victoria, British Columbia, we acknowledge the traditional territories of the Lkwungen (Esquimalt, and Songhees), Malahat, Pacheedaht, Scia'new, T'Sou-ke and W̱SÁNEĆ (Pauquachin, Tsartlip, Tsawout, Tseycum) peoples.

We acknowledge the financial support of the Government of Canada through the Canada Book Fund and the Canada Council for the Arts, and of the province of British Columbia through the British Columbia Arts Council and the Book Publishing Tax Credit.

Disclaimer

The information provided reflects the authors' experiences and opinions, and is designed to help you make informed decisions about your body and health. The suggestions for specific foods, exercises, and medications in this program are not intended to replace appropriate or necessary medical care.

Before starting any exercise regimen, always consult your physician. Ask for a physical stress test. If any recommendations in this book contradict your physician's advice, be sure to consult them before proceeding. The mention of specific products, organizations, companies, or authorities in this book does not imply endorsement by the authors, nor does the mention of specific products, organizations, companies, nor authorities imply that they endorse this book. The authors disclaim any liability of loss, personal or otherwise, that is incurred as a result, directly or indirectly, of the use and applications of any of the contents of this publication.

Dedicated to our husbands, Mike and Paul.

You never conquer a mountain. You stand on the summit a few brief minutes
and then the wind blows away your footprints.
– Arlene Blum

Contents

Photo by Michael Sarver

IF I WASN'T GOING TO MAKE IT,
IT WOULD BE FOR SOME OTHER REASON.

I watched the ground from the tiny window in the small plane. I was surveying the African parkland – flat and brown with ribbons and haphazard patches of green – looking for a single ice-capped mound somewhere beneath the aircraft. After scrunching my body to see under the plane's propeller, something caught my eye. My spine straightened all the way to my neck, my chin tilting up and to the left. My gaze settled and then widened upon her. Kibo. Kilimanjaro's highest peak, breaking through a layer of cloud worn like a dusty Victorian ruff. I reeled my gaze back to the aircraft and realized the mountaintop was practically in line with the plane's wing.

Damn. That's high. Tugging on my husband's arm, I pressed backward into my seat, offering him a chance to look.

Paul and I had got married several months earlier, a winter wedding in the Canadian Rockies, and we'd accepted donations for the trek from our tribe of friends and family as wedding gifts. It didn't add up to enough, but my new mother-in-law – whose generosity knows no bounds (and who was not-so-subtly eager to be a grandmother) – kindly subsidized the missing chunk of cash to expedite the trip. This was the start of our Kilimanjaro honeymoon. Mountains are an obvious but apt metaphor. This trip would be a preview of how we'd manage the adventure that will be our lives together.

My husband doesn't remember what his reaction was when he saw Kili for the first time from the plane. This boggles my mind. *How could you not remember your first time seeing Kilimanjaro?!* But then I remember what else his mind was likely preoccupied with.

You see, heeding our trainer Angela's advice to walk, walk, walk, walk, we had opted for a few days of practice hikes in Jasper National Park in the week before our departure. Fortunate to have mountain trails a half-day's drive away, we picked a few that we thought best mimicked Kilimanjaro's gradual progression of difficulty. On our last hike, coming down through fields of wild flowers on Mount Edith Cavell, we got caught in a downpour that came about too quickly for us to get out all our rain gear. We returned home to Edmonton later that night, our boots drenched.

Because my husband is thoughtful, he pulled the insoles out of my boots so they could dry before we left. Because my husband is humble, he didn't tell me about his good deed. Because my husband pulled my insoles out of my boots and didn't tell me, we got all the way to our first connection before I realized that the reason my boots felt funny when I walked out the door on the morning of our departure wasn't because of nerves. It was because the insoles I had spent several kilometres breaking in were sitting on our shoe rack at home.

I think Paul doesn't remember his first Kili sighting because he was in his own head trying to figure out how we were going to acquire insoles for my boots before the climb. No stores sold them at

Toronto Pearson International, and there were no stores to even look through in the underbelly of the Addis Ababa, Ethiopia, airport, either, where we waited for our second connecting flight. Some things in this world are indeed still impossible, and shipping my insoles from Alberta to Tanzania in fewer than three days is one of those things. (We checked.)

Staring at Kilimanjaro from a plane full of other trekkers, I wasn't concerned about the insoles. I had googled a mall in Moshi, and knowing the number of hikers going through every year, I was sure there would be a store that sold all sorts of gear. The fact that I imagined an MEC in the middle of Moshi seems ridiculous to me, now, because there would not be one in the "mall," which turned out to be a small, half-bare-shelved general grocer. But no way would the universe put me on the path to this mountain if it was all going to be nixed because of a couple of missing shoe cushions. No. If I wasn't going to make it, it would be for some other reason.

There were times before leaving when I almost allowed anxiety to get the best of me. Over thirty thousand people attempt the climb every year, but nearly half don't summit. And – every year – a handful of people die in the attempt. Was this a foolish choice? Selfish, for sure, given that the goal to climb Kilimanjaro was one that Paul hadn't considered until I brought it up. But now we were on the plane, the trip paid for by people back home waiting for that "we made it!" Facebook post.

Did we prepare well enough? I thought, evaluating my journey up to that point while squinting at the mountain, trying to spot tiny fluorescent dots of people moving about it. I had completed most of my weekly workouts and stair sessions, but the hours-long walks with our dog happened maybe only a third of the time, if I was being honest. We did those practice hikes, and they went well, but I was beat by the end of them – and that was only three days at less than 2800 metres. This trip would be eight days and top out at just under 6000 metres.

The *ding* of the intercom and the captain's voice brought my awareness back to the plane as we descended toward Kilimanjaro International Airport.

This book is a Kilimanjaro travelogue, but more important, it's a guide to how Paul and I prepared ourselves for our most gruelling physical challenge to date. Paul and I went from varying degrees of fitness to being in the best shape of our lives for the climb. You'll see us at our first workout, run from bears with us in the Rockies, and, of course, trek up Kilimanjaro too.

Sure, I could keep it suspenseful and let the question hang: do I make it to the top? I'll tell you right now, not everyone on our team does, but – insoles or no insoles – I do.

INTRODUCING YOUR TRAINER:
ANGELA DEJONG

I grew up in small-town Alberta with flat farmland as far as the eye can see – not the environment you'd think would foster my early obsession with Africa and volcanoes. As a child, I'd never been to Africa, but the images I'd cut out of the *National Geographic* magazines at school left a mark on my heart and a never-ending dream to visit one day. As an adult I've been fortunate to combine my passions for fitness and travel, and to make a career out of helping others reach new heights in fitness and health, and in terms of elevation. I've been a personal trainer and nutrition coach since 2001. Over the last fifteen years I have trekked and climbed mountains all over the world, focussing on African peaks and volcanoes for the last decade. I've summited the highest peak in each country of the African continent that has a mountain over 3000 metres. Mount Kilimanjaro was the second summit I reached, and a decade later, I remember it like it was yesterday. I've also prepared many clients for successful treks, including Machu Picchu, Peru; Rwenzoris, Uganda; Mount Everest Base Camp, Nepal; Mount Robson, Canada; Mount Adams, USA; Mount Aconcagua, Argentina; and, of course, Mount Kilimanjaro, Tanzania.

In 2014, after I completed a draft of my first book, *Reality Fitness*, I contacted my co-author for this book, Erinne, to inquire about editing it. Asking a stranger to evaluate the words I had put my heart and soul into for years was scary and intimidating. Never one to run from fear, however,

I sent Erinne the three-hundred-plus-page document and waited for an email from her. *What will she think about my book?* I was nervous and terrified that I'd look foolish for even considering it worth publishing. I've never felt more vulnerable. A few weeks later, she asked that we meet face-to-face to discuss my writing and the publishing process. I make it sound like an in-person meeting was no big deal, but I was freaking out.

I walked into a local coffee shop, wearing stretchy fitness gear, carrying a water bottle and a backpack. I scanned the room and set my eyes on an intelligent-looking gal behind a computer screen, wearing funky glasses, her hair piled on top of her head in a bun that had a pencil pierced through it, and a lovely scarf draped over her shoulders. *That has to be her!* By appearances alone, it would seem that we'd have nothing in common, but our conversation flowed with ease, and it became evident that we had more similarities than either of us might have anticipated. Erinne expressed her love of mountains and her desire to do more travelling – Africa was high on her list. I'm sure my eyes lit up when she said this, and it naturally led to a discussion about climbing Kilimanjaro. This conversation was the beginning of something very special. That day we agreed, Erinne would help edit and publish *Reality Fitness*, while I would prepare Erinne and Paul (her fiancé, then) to reach the highest point in Africa. With the trade set, I think we both had an inkling that while working on one book we'd be gathering the building blocks for a second.

And so here we are with that second book. *Polepole* is intended to physically and mentally prepare you to trek Kilimanjaro or to take on any other multi-day, non-technical mountain hike around the world (not mountaineering, but walkable, hiking-boot and/or crampon routes that require little to no rope work). My part in this book provides you with trekking-specific workouts that are critical to reaching the summit and making it back down safely. Erinne's part gives you a first-hand account of not only journeying up and down the mountain but also of what it took to prepare in the months and weeks leading up to the climb.

Trekking high-altitude mountains is no easy task. Nearly 50 per cent of people who attempt to summit Mount Kilimanjaro do not succeed as a result of injury, altitude sickness, or lack of preparation. It is important to give yourself adequate time to train and that you take the training seriously. Cramming months of preparation into the final weeks before your departure can leave you in a dangerous situation. Trekking mountains is different than running a road race, where you have luxuries around you like the comfort of your own bed at night and access to nearby hospitals. When you trek, you want your body to be as physically fit as possible, not just to accomplish your summit goal but to get back down safely. The good news is that you've already taken a step in the right direction with this book. *Polepole* (pronounced po-lay po-lay) is a Swahili term used in East Africa meaning "slowly, slowly." Guides and porters say this repeatedly while assisting trekkers to the summit. If you are preparing for Kilimanjaro, or any another peak in East Africa, you will be very familiar with this saying by the time you have completed Day One of your hike. But *polepole* is not just a phrase you use on the mountain. It also applies to your training.

The training program laid out in this book will provide you with enough time and incremental progress to adequately prepare for the climb, regardless of your starting fitness level. The mountain-hiking experience is so much more enjoyable when you're feeling strong, fit, healthy, physically and mentally capable, and confident in your ability to endure a trek. Embarking on an adventure like this one will do more than get you a stamp in your passport and a certificate for your wall. It can change your life. For that reason, I am so excited for you and your journey, and I am so thankful that you've chosen us to help you along the way. Take things *polepole*, and enjoy the process.

How to Use this Program

Arriving at the top of a mountain of any height is a proud moment. Summiting the highest point on the African continent, at nearly 6000 metres high, is exhilarating. It is true, however, that anything worth doing isn't easy. Following a consistent training program will be necessary to ensure you have enough cardiovascular fitness, muscular endurance in your legs and upper body (to carry your daypack), and muscular strength to climb up and over larger rock formations.

This program is divided into three phases: Beginner, Intermediate and Advanced. The phase where you begin will depend on your starting fitness level (which I will help you determine in the coming pages). In this book, each workout is presented in summary. (Jump ahead to page 21 to take a quick glimpse of the first one, if you'd like.) Detailed descriptions and photos of the exercises are at the back of the book.

I've chosen the most valuable exercises specifically geared to long-distance trekking. The volume and intensity of the workouts gradually increases as the program moves forward, and the duration of workouts and the training exercises will also increase.

But first things first.

Figure Out Where and When to Start

This book is designed to be useful for people of any fitness level. As such, you will need to evaluate your personal level before beginning the workouts. The more fit you are to start, the fewer months of training you can get away with, and you can begin with more intense workouts. The three starting points are detailed below.

Beginner Fitness Level: Nine Months of Training

If two or more of the following criteria apply to you, start with this training category.

- You have never hiked a mountain before.
- You currently do fewer than two sessions (30 minutes, minimum) of cardiovascular/aerobic workouts a week.
- You currently do fewer than two sessions of strength-training workouts a week.
- You have exercised for less than six months with regular activity.
- You take fewer than 10,000 steps a day, on average.

If you fall into this category, start your training a minimum of nine months before your departure at the Beginner Training Phase (page 19).

Intermediate Level: Six to Nine Months of Training

If two or more of the following criteria apply to you, start with this training category.

- You have never hiked a mountain at high elevation but have some experience walking outside on uneven ground/trails or lower-elevation mountains.
- You currently do at least three sessions (30 minutes, minimum) of cardiovascular/aerobic workouts a week.

- You currently do at least two sessions of strength-training workouts a week.
- You have exercised consistently at least two times a week for the past twelve months.
- You take at least 10,000 steps a day, on average.

If you fall into this category, start your training a minimum of six months before your departure at the Intermediate Training Phase (page 41).

Advanced Level:
Three to Six Months of Training

If two or more of the following criteria apply to you, start with this training category.

- You have never hiked a mountain at high elevation but have some experience walking outside on uneven ground/trails or lower-elevation mountains.
- You currently do at least four sessions (30 minutes, minimum) of cardiovascular/aerobic workouts a week.
- You currently do at least four sessions of strength-training workouts a week.
- You have exercised consistently at least four times a week for the past twelve months.
- You take at least 10,000 steps per day, on average.

If you fall into this category, start your training a minimum of three months before your departure at the Advanced Training Phase (page 69).

It is not critical that you select one category and stay within it. These are guidelines to give you a starting point to work from. There are many other variables at work when it comes to fitness. If you find after a two-week period the program volume (time needed to train) is too aggressive or not challenging enough based on your previous training routine, make the switch to the appropriate category. The reason for testing a category for two weeks before making the switch is simply to give you time to know if an adjustment is necessary.

Often clients are very eager at the beginning of any new workout plan and then burn out if they start with too much at the get-go. There is ample time for preparation, so making a change two weeks into the program is 100 per cent okay. Best to make the change early on rather than two months into the program.

Remember that regardless of where you start, Erinne and Paul's journey is woven throughout all phases of this program. It's entertaining and contains a ton of helpful lessons she learned both in training and while on her trip. Don't miss it!

Gather Your Fitness Equipment and Pick Your Space

There are several places where you can work out. Getting a gym membership is an easy way to ensure you will have all the equipment you need. If you prefer to work out at home, make sure you have the following:

- A bench or sturdy chair;
- A fitness exercise ball;
- Dumbbells ranging from light to heavy weight (5–40 lb [4.5–9 kg]; requirements vary depending on fitness level);
- Access to a large hill or stairs outside (the higher the better); and

- Access to a treadmill and/or a stair-climber (not mandatory if you are comfortable training outside).

Equipment required for specific phases of this program is listed at the start of each section.

Keep in mind that by the advanced phase you will want to have the boots and backpack you are planning to take on your hike. Using them while training is the perfect way to make sure they are broken-in well.

Review the Terminology

Your workouts will consist of exercises (movements) organized into multiple series of several sets of several reps. Some of those exercises will require light or moderate weight in the form of dumbbells.

Wait, what? If the above paragraph has you confused, the following definitions should help.

Reps: Short for repetition, this is the number of times you complete a movement. For example, if the workout asks for 12 reps of bicep curls, lift the weight 12 times.

Set: One round of the specified number of reps. Your workouts will require multiple sets (or rounds) of the exercises.

Series: A systemized compilation of exercises or grouping of exercises. Exercises are to be performed in the order they are listed and then repeated for the number of sets indicated.

Weight: The amount of weight you are using to perform an exercise. Sometimes this is your body weight, and other times you will require additional resistance using dumbbells.

- *Light weight:* Weight you can lift 15 times or more with ease.
- *Moderate weight:* Weight you can lift at least 10–12 times, with the last 2 repetitions being a challenge but doable with proper form.

Take a Before Pic!

Some of my clients like to take photos of their training along the way to document their journey to the summit. While your goal is not about how you look, your body is likely to change throughout this process. These pictures could be a nice addition to the photo book or slide show that you will hopefully create with the incredible pictures from your climb. Of course, this is not for everyone, but it might be for you, and you will feel proud of your accomplishment, regardless.

Walking

On average, you're looking at five to six hours of walking each day that you're on Kilimanjaro (more than twice that on summit day). It's critical to prepare your muscles, ligaments, tendons and minds for that kind of wear and tear. Therefore, along with your workouts, I've included regular walking sessions. The walking worked into your training schedules is designed to build up your stamina gradually. Walking too far, too fast can lead to overtraining and possible injury. Walks will start small (thirty minutes, at the beginning) and then build until you're walking for three hours, in your hiking boots, carrying weight in your daypack.

How to Use the Training Schedule

Each training phase includes a sample calendar of workouts. The schedule is designed to provide a balanced routine that covers strength training, muscular endurance training, cardiovascular training and rest. It details which workouts to do, when, and when to get your walks in. You are not expected to follow the calendar exactly as written. Maybe weekends are a better time for you to work out, and Tuesdays are a no-go, for example. This is not a problem. Print off your own calendar (or open your calendar app) and add in your workouts and walks on the days that work for you. Just ensure you do not miss any workouts or walking sessions, and make sure to complete them in the same order as written in the sample calendar.

This training will prepare you both physically and mentally for the climb. If you can complete the months of training necessary, you will be ready to endure the long hours of walking, for multiple days, in an environment with practically half the effective oxygen you're used to.

Let's get started!

BEGINNER TRAINING PHASE

Welcome to the start of your Kilimanjaro training! The next nine months will be a fun challenge, physically and mentally. This set of workouts provides you with all the foundational movements for weight training. Your balance, muscular endurance and cardiovascular system will all be challenged.

Since these workouts are not tailored to your individual fitness level, it is important that you listen to your body and place yourself in the appropriate training category. If after two weeks you are finding the beginner workouts to be too easy (you are able to perform the exercises with correct technique and are not challenged) please move on to the intermediate workouts, but continue to follow the beginner walking schedule. Walking too far, too fast can lead to overtraining and possible injury. It is best to ease yourself in for as long as you can, especially since your hiking boots and backpacks will come into play later.

Equipment Required

Equipment required for this phase includes the following:

• A variety of dumbbells ranging in weight.

Kilimanjaro by the Numbers

Each workout in this set is named by a number with special significance to Kilimanjaro.

Workout Index

Beginner Training Schedule (1–9 Months)

Week	Monday	Tuesday	Wednesday	Thursday	Friday	Saturday	Sunday
1	OFF	1889	OFF	30-min walk	OFF	OFF	30-min walk
2	OFF	1889	OFF	45-min walk	OFF	OFF	45-min walk
3	OFF	1889	OFF	4:56	OFF	OFF	60-min walk
4	OFF	1889	OFF	4:56	OFF	OFF	60-min walk
5	OFF	1889	OFF	4:56	OFF	OFF	75-min walk
6	OFF	1889	OFF	4:56	OFF	OFF	75-min walk
7	OFF	4:56	OFF	7/88	OFF	OFF	75-min walk
8	OFF	4:56	OFF	7/88	30-min walk	OFF	75-min walk
9	OFF	7/88	OFF	5895	30-min walk	OFF	90-min walk
10	OFF	7/88	OFF	5895	45-min walk	OFF	75-min walk
11	OFF	7/88	OFF	5895	45-min walk	OFF	75-min walk
12	OFF	7/88	OFF	5895	45-min walk	OFF	75-min walk

Off Days: Ensure you avoid strenuous activities on OFF days. A light walk or a light stretching class is okay.

Beginner Training Warm-Up Summary

All your workouts should start with a warm-up, which transitions your body from a cold, static state to a warm, mobile state while gently raising your heart rate. For this stage of training, you have a choice of two cardiovascular activities.

1. Treadmill Incline Walk

Walk on the treadmill at an incline of 10–15 (or outside if a treadmill is not available) for five to ten minutes at a pace that allows you to carry on a conversation with someone but leaves you slightly out of breath. Your heart rate should increase slightly, and you may begin to sweat a little bit. It is okay to lean slightly forward at the hips while walking at an incline, but avoid bending too far forward. If you are unable to stay upright or must hang on to the treadmill to maintain your pace, decrease the speed of the treadmill to keep an upright walking posture.

2. Up and Down Stairs

Walk, jog or run up and down a flight of stairs for five minutes. The objective is to pace yourself so you can maintain movement for the length of time without stopping. Your heart rate should increase slightly, and you may begin to sweat a little bit.

1889
Beginner Workout One

*On October 6, 1889, German geologist Hans Meyer, along
with Austrian mountaineer Ludwig Purtscheller and local
Chagga teen Yohana Kinyala Lauwo, made the first recorded
summit of Mount Kilimanjaro after a series of attempts
by other foreigners. Some suggest that Lauwo summitted
the mountain earlier, but his climb was not recorded.*

Warm-up		
Stairs or treadmill walk	5-10 mins	Light to moderate pace
Series One: Repeat the series twice		
1. Squats	15	Light weight
2. Stationary lunges	10/side	
3. Stairs	2 mins	
Series Two: Repeat the series twice		
1. Single leg bicep curls	10/side	Light weight
2. Plank off hands with alternating knee-pulls to the chest	10/side	
3. Stairs	2 mins	
Series Three: Repeat the series once		
1. Walking	15 mins	Light to moderate pace

AFRICA? YES. LET'S GO.

I can thank my Grade 8 Social Studies teacher for my interest in travel. He was the one who wheeled in the TV during our Brazil unit to show us an episode of what was then called *Lonely Planet*. From that day on I made a habit of catching the episodes every week at home, curling up with a bowl of oatmeal and brown sugar every time because, to thirteen-year-old me, that was a traveller's meal. My life goal became to land on all seven continents. In Africa, I imagined, I'd be in tan khakis, drenched in that fuchsia-orange glow of the sun lying low on a dusty horizon.

Fast forward to my early twenties. I had travelled a bit in Europe and Central America and was itching for my next journey. That's when a work manager come friend, Connie, suggested we climb Kilimanjaro together with a group she'd heard on the radio that was looking for more members. Here was a chance to cross Africa off my list of continents to visit. It didn't matter that I couldn't tell you how high Kilimanjaro was, nor that it bordered Kenya and Tanzania, countries I couldn't point to on a map.

Africa?

Yes. Let's go.

As the idea started to gel, several issues cropped up. First, I had second thoughts about how we'd get along with the group from the radio. See, the business Connie and I worked for was a home-party, "adult novelty" company. We sold vibrators. It was a great gig, and I was great at it. The group on the radio, however, was a religious group from small-town Alberta. And while my experience in

the industry left me knowing these church ladies had more going on behind closed doors and in their nightstands than they let on, outwardly Connie and I would likely need to keep all details about our work secret. The idea felt dishonest – a couple of sex-toy saleswomen infiltrating a church mission for the sake of getting to Africa. But also, I just didn't have the money to go. Not even aware that the cost of the trip could run upwards of $10,000, I hardly had money for the immunizations to get me started. So when Connie called me to schedule an appointment at the travel clinic, I broke the news to her. She also didn't end up going. An email slip-up led to her working life being found out, and she was respectfully uninvited by the group. But years later, she came to our wedding and contributed to our Kilimanjaro fund while reaffirming her intention to accomplish the journey one day herself.

Now I'm getting ahead of myself, though, because by the time of our wedding, Paul and I had already started training. On October 22, 2014, Paul and I drove to Angela's home gym for our first workout. I was terrified! Mostly of embarrassment and failure. Also, we were running behind. I pulled her number up on my phone, listed in my contacts as "Kili" because "Angela" was already taken, and let her know we were three minutes away.

Paul was a relatively fit guy, having been committed to the gym for a while and playing with his men's league hockey team as a goalie several times a week. Meanwhile, I had gone to the gym on and off since high school, but mostly off. I took a similar approach to yoga. I snowboarded a handful of times a year. That's it. No set regimen in a long while, and definitely no team sports. The last time I had tried to run, my lungs seized up halfway down the block, and then I coughed and wheezed for days. And here I was thinking I'd be able to climb the highest mountain in Africa? Surely Angela would see right through my façade, and she would have to tell me gently that I was too unfit now and likely incapable of becoming fit enough to summit by the time our honeymoon came around.

When we arrived I masked my nerves with questions. Questions about her house and private gym, questions about her cat, questions about...

"So, what would you say are the best kind of socks to wear? I've got regular socks and ankle socks."

Socks?! They say there are no stupid questions, but really...socks? Leave it to Ang to take all my questions seriously. (The answer, by the way, is sport socks, which will at least not fall under your heel while you're moving.) Thing is, she knew how I felt. Angela came into my life as a client of my editing and publishing consulting business. Up until this point, Angela was "author" and I was "editor." She made herself vulnerable via her manuscript, which she trusted me to judge and critique (constructively, of course). I was comfortable in this position of knowledge and authority. The day of our first workout, our roles were reversed, and I was putting myself out there – rolls and all – leaving myself open for judgement and criticism. Frankly, I didn't feel like I was coming to the table with a lot. We were quick to acknowledge the parallels in our positions of service provider and client. Between her book and my body, egos were at stake for both of us. In that sense, we were even.

The workout began. And after all that buildup, it wasn't so bad, and neither was I. It started with a gentle warm-up on the treadmill, and I was surprised to come off it with clear lungs. (Ang explained that the temperature of the air can affect a run.) Then we got into some basic exercises. Squats and jump squats, some lunges, some walkouts. Questions abounded as I dissected everything from foot placement to when and how I should breathe. I felt good and encouraged. Somehow Paul was sweating more than me by the end of it.

I didn't lift a single dumbbell that day. Everything I needed to do, I could do with a mat on the floor. Or without, even. We left knowing that the workout summary would be uploaded to a

Dropbox folder, and Ang gave us a printed calendar that detailed the days we were to work out and the days we were to take our dog Nyx out for a long walk.

I needn't have worried as much as I did on that car ride over. I made it through, and contrary to what I imagined, there was no criticism at all. I would discover that to be one of Angela's best qualities: never judgemental and abundantly compassionate. Even when I inevitably apologized for my physical state, Angela didn't allow me to feel shame. It didn't matter what my fitness level used to be like or even what it was when I walked through her door that day. What mattered was the goal – Kilimanjaro – and that I was taking the right steps to be prepared for it, starting with those first few on the treadmill. None of Angela's clients who'd attempted Kilimanjaro thus far had failed to summit (no pressure), and she would make sure that – *polepole* – Paul and I would be ready to take it on.

Thus began our Friday morning workout ritual. Me, my husband and Angela. And sometimes her cat Larry.

4:56
Beginner Workout Two

*On August 13, 2014, Swiss runner Karl Egloff ran to the summit
of Kilimanjaro in 4 hours 56 minutes: the fastest ascent to date.*

Warm-up		
Stairs or treadmill walk	5 mins	Light to moderate pace
Series One: Repeat the series twice		
1. Squats	15	Moderate weight
2. Alternating back lunges	10/side	Light weight
3. Stairs	3 mins	
4. Plank off elbows	30 secs	
Series Two: Repeat the series twice		
1. Lateral shuffles	1 min/side	
2. Stationary side lunge	12/side	Light weight
3. Jumping-jack planks	30	
Series Three: Repeat the series once		
1. Walking	30 mins	Moderate pace

WITH EVERY WORKOUT,
MY BODY CHANGED.

Paul and I lived in Old Strathcona, one of Edmonton's older and trendier neighbourhoods, close to the University of Alberta and the Saskatchewan River valley. Decades-old trees provide shady canopies for the streets in summer. The homes are a mix of skinny infill builds and homes like ours, what real-estate agents refer to as "character homes" (read: "tiny AF"). The space worked for us, though. We had three (albeit small) rooms. One for us to sleep in, one for my office, and the "flex" room that sometimes housed an air mattress for travelling friends but at that point in time stored all our wedding accoutrements.

By late fall, the big trees were almost bare and had turned that brown-grey colour they have while awaiting snow. Both Paul and I were fortunate in our work lives to have a lot of control over our schedules. Between my freelance editing and music teaching, and his contract-based work as a massage therapist, we had the flexibility to shape our schedules to make our training sessions and workouts fit. Paul, who already had a membership he used frequently, preferred to work out at the gym. I, on the other hand, preferred privacy and chose our flex room, pushing all our centrepieces and fabrics and candles up along the outside wall, which left me with a rectangle of about forty square feet. Small, but it was all I needed.

Every month we posted the calendar Angela provided us to the pantry door in our kitchen. Each day was marked with either the specific workout we were to complete or "Walk 1 hr," which we dutifully crossed off as we completed them. Sometimes workouts happened a day or two later than intended, but they generally happened, and we reported back to Angela at our training session every Friday.

On workout days at home, I would run up and down the small flight of stairs that led to our basement neighbour's door to warm up (unless she was home, in which case I'd lateral shuffle back and forth along our hallway). Returning to the flex room, I'd spread out a yoga mat in line with the window that looked out over our backyard, and then start the series Angela had designed specifically for me that week: lunges, planks, curls, jacks, whatever. All the while, an old-school hip-hop playlist streamed from a small Bluetooth speaker in the corner. Over time, this tiny space became my micro-gym (a literal flex room, if you'll allow me the pun) with the addition of elastic bands and dumbbells as Angela introduced them into our workouts.

What blew my mind in this phase of our training was realizing how effective "simple" exercises could be ("if you do them with correct technique!" Ang would like to emphasize). I was always shocked at how quickly squats could get my heart rate going. I'd pop into the bathroom to adjust a contact lens and be caught off guard by the flush red of my cheeks. For years I'd skim through magazines and not even bother with any of the exercise tips, be it for toned arms or a flat stomach. While I would've liked those things, the moves seemed way too simple to actually work. Really? Jump like this thirty times, lift that twelve times, and repeat for three? That's it? I didn't buy it.

While the promise was never a flat stomach, Ang's moves were no different than the ones I'd seen in magazines, and we ran through them in similar sets of reps. With every workout, my body changed. My strength became noticeable in the everyday things, like getting up and down from a seated position or carrying my groceries inside. I came to realize that even a twenty-minute series a few times a week accumulates to have a significant impact on strength and well-being. Ang's workouts were more than twenty minutes each, of course. But keeping it simple and working out from home, I could still squeeze a whole workout into less than forty-five minutes.

For the most part, I enjoyed working out. Truly! I learned to relish the feeling of my body temperature rising and my heart rate increasing. There was this one workout, though, that I absolutely *hated*. (I think it was the high-knees that did it, maybe my least-favourite exercise.) Gearing up for exercise on days with this particular workout on deck took a lot of will power. It was during this workout, one day, that I got a call from one of my bridesmaids with questions about my bridal shower.

"Can I call you in about thirty minutes?" I asked her. "I'm just mid-workout. If I stop now, I'm not going back."

"Good for you, girl. You're gonna look fabulous in your dress!"

She was not wrong. On my wedding day, I looked fabulous. I would be lying to say that toning up for the big day was not also a consideration when enlisting Angela's help for Kilimanjaro. But as I hung up and returned to the workout (fucking high-knees!), I recognized that I was exercising more than just my body when I pushed myself through the parts I hated. There were bound to be times on Kilimanjaro that I would not enjoy, times where I'd want to quit. In pushing myself now, I was building a habit to push beyond my comfort zone, both physically and mentally.

All this said, there were days I just *couldn't* bring myself to do it. The first time I missed a workout completely, I arrived at our training session prepared with my confession. "I tried," I told Angela. "I even put on all my gear and went into the room. But I just couldn't make my body move." I awaited my penance, but there was none. Angela was happy even with my intention and was understanding. Sometimes the will to work out just isn't in us. As long as it didn't happen too often, a missed workout wouldn't derail my progress, and I should stop feeling guilty.

7/88
Beginner Workout Three

In 2008, when Keats Boyd was just seven years old, he summited Kilimanjaro and became the youngest to reach the top. In 2018, two other seven-year-olds, Cash Callahan and Montannah Kenney, followed in Boyd's footsteps and reached the top of the mountain. In 2017, at the age of 88, Dr. Fred Distelhorst became the oldest person to reach the summit.

Warm-up		
Stairs or treadmill walk	5–10 mins	Light to moderate pace
Series One: Repeat the series twice		
1. Front squats	15	Light weight
2. Walking lunges	1 min	Light weight
3. Walkouts	10	
Series Two: Repeat the series twice		
1. Wide–narrow jump squats	15 each	
2. Glute bridge	1 min	
3. Single foot hops	25/side	
4. Push-ups off knees	10	
5. 3-point mid row	12/side	Moderate weight
Series Three: Repeat the series once		
1. Walking	30 mins	Moderate pace

Fuel Your Body: A Note on Nutrition

Trekking Kilimanjaro is an athletic feat. To get the most out of your training, I strongly suggest that you eat like an athlete does. The more optimally your body is fuelled and hydrated, the more energy it will have, the better it will perform, and the quicker it will recover to be ready for the next day of training.

A balanced nutrition program for someone training to climb a mountain includes:

- drinking at least three litres of water each day, more if you are training outside in the heat;
- eating a snack or meal every three to four hours during the day to optimize your energy levels;
- eating one serving of Grade A protein at every meal, and one serving of Grade A or B protein at every snack;
- eating two servings of vegetables at every meal (one healthy handful = one serving, two servings is about half your plate);
- eating one serving of grains or other carbohydrates at every meal; and
- eating one serving of healthy fat as part of every meal and snack.

Put another way, each *meal* should include: one serving of Grade A protein, two servings of vegetables, one serving of grains or other carbohydrates, and one serving of healthy fat.

Each *snack* should include: one serving of Grade A or Grade B protein and one serving of healthy fat.

You can find examples of healthy options for your food choices in the charts on page 30.

Having plenty of water and a variety of carbohydrates, protein-rich foods, and healthy fats enables your body to perform at its best when you are exercising. The healthier your body is leading up to the trek, the better your chances are of making it.

If you would like a more comprehensive nutrition program, you can find additional information in my book *Reality Fitness*, or check out www.realityfitnessbook.com for details about my online nutrition-coaching program.

Strategic Eating for Training

While it's beneficial to have a healthy and balanced eating program, there are also two strategic ways to eat that will help you make the most of your training.

1. Eat a meal one hour pre-workout and one hour post-workout to support muscle retention. Slow, steady-state activity (like running, walking stairs and hiking) can cause your body to metabolize muscle tissue. Eating lean protein with carbohydrates before and after your workouts will help prevent this.

2. Eat snacks during walking sessions that last longer than an hour to maintain your energy levels and assist you with your performance. These snacks should be between 150 and 250 calories and can be any combination of protein, fats, and/or carbs. Choose foods that will agree with your stomach during activity.

Healthy Options Nutrition Charts

Grade A Protein Sources (Best Sources)

Source	Amount per Serving
Beef	3–4 oz
Bison	3–4 oz
Chicken	3–4 oz
Cottage cheese	1/2 c
Crab	3–4 oz
Eggs	2
Egg whites	4
Fish	3–4 oz
Plain Greek yogurt	1/2 c
Protein powder (Whey, casein)	1 scoop
Salmon	3–4 oz
Scallops	5 large
Shrimp	5 large
Tofu	1/2 c
Turkey	3–4 oz

Grade B Protein Sources (Next-Best Sources)

Source	Amount per Serving
Beans	1/2 c
Edamame	1/2 c
Farro	1/2 c
Hemp hearts	2 tbsp
Lentils	1/2 c
Nuts	1/4 c
Nut butters	1 tbsp
Seeds	2 tbsp

Best Grains and Other Carbohydrate Sources

Source	Amount per Serving
Ancient grains (amaranth, barley, farro, millet, quinoa, spelt, teff)	1/3 c uncooked
Apples	1
Bananas	1
Berries	1/2 c
Bread	1 slice
Brown rice	1/2 c cooked
Grapefruit	1
Oatmeal	1/2 c
Sweet vegetables	3/4 c
Tortilla	1 (6-in)

Best Fat Sources

Source	Amount per Serving
Avocado	2 tbsp
Cheese (dairy and dairy free)	1 oz
Flax (ground)	1 tbsp
Nuts (unsalted, unroasted)	1/4 c
Nut butters	1 tbsp
Oils (coconut, grape-seed, olive)	1 tbsp
Salad dressings (oil- or yogurt-based are best)	1 tbsp

Hiking Snacks on Your Trek

When you're hiking at high altitude and in cold weather, you need a great deal of energy. Every individual requires a different number of calories when hiking. As a guideline, bring one snack with you for every 1.5–2 hours of trekking (200–300 calories per snack). This is in addition to your meals. The average day of walking on Kilimanjaro is approximately 6 hours. Multiply the number of days you are planning to hike by three so you can pack enough snacks, and then toss in a couple extra, just in case. If you do not eat them all, that is okay. It is better to carry a few more snacks than you think you might need than not having enough energy to make it to the summit, and it's also good to have the extras in case of an emergency.

Types of Hiking Snacks

As with any time during your training, your trekking snacks are not treats to be eaten at any time. Instead, they are key parts of your hike, there to help you replace the calories you have lost so you have continuous energy to keep hiking. I'm a bona fide health nut and like to promote healthy living, but I am fully aware of the impact altitude has on appetite. Altitude can affect your desire to eat. Choose the snacks you take wisely. Eating *anything* is better than not eating. If that means you can stomach the idea of eating a chocolate bar but not dried fruit, have the chocolate bar. You will need the caloric energy to hike every day. When you are on that final stretch to the summit – it's early in the morning, your body is so tired and you are wondering why you wanted to endure this in the first place – pulling out that snack, a comfort from home, can be the difference between making it and not making it.

Snack and Exercise Tip

Use your long walking sessions as a test: What snacks provide you the most energy? Which ones make your stomach feel good? What is easy to chew? (Yes, this is a factor when you're hiking.) Having this information in advance will help you plan what snacks to take for your trek so you feel confident in the energy they provide.

Hiking Snack Ideas

Following are some of my suggestions, along with some client favourites!

- Sunflower seeds
- Chocolate-hazelnut spread and pretzels
- Trail mix
- Pre-packaged Rice Krispie squares
- Granola
- Cookies or crackers
- Pepperoni sticks or beef jerky
- Gummy candies
- Chocolate bars
- Energy/protein bars
- Nuts and mini peanut-butter packets
- Dried fruit and dried fruit bars
- Ginger chews

Depending on your time, many of these snacks can be purchased in Africa. If, however, you have little time to stock up, or you prefer a certain brand of food, bring your snacks from home. Be sure they are in sealed packages, are airplane/border friendly and are in your checked luggage.

I ABSORBED NUTRITION HABITS
AS IF THROUGH OSMOSIS.

"Okay, let's see what you're eating," said the naturopath, peering up at me from above his glasses.

I had come at Paul's urging to see if there was something I could do for my "pseudo-asthma," what I called my wheezing reaction any time I ran outdoors. It was never an issue any other time, and workouts with Ang seemed to be immune, but my concern was not taking a *potentially* real problem seriously and then being caught on the mountain in a full-on attack, needing an inhaler and not having one. I would check in with my family physician, too, but having been on breathing meds before and hating them, I was willing to give anything else a shot first.

The meeting went poorly. I found the naturopath cocky and patronizing, and I mentally checked out by the time he started mansplaining the signs of ovulation to me. But as I drove home fuming, outlining in my head how I would tell the day's story to Paul, the question about eating stuck out.

"Okay, let's see what you're eating. Uh huh. So. Coffee, milk and meat? That's it?"

I explained that in filling out the extensive intake form I'd merely jotted down the first few things that came to mind when asked what I ate and drank regularly. I'd moved on and neglected to come back to the question. When I stopped to think about what I would add, though, that short list wasn't far from the whole truth, perhaps missing only foods like cheese, granola bars, bread and gummy candies. What I ate wasn't something I had time to think about. Most

dinnertimes I was on the road between the homes of my music students. I hadn't ever learned to cook well for myself, either, beyond boiling store-bought tortellini or making a wrap out of packaged chicken fingers and pre-made dressing when I got home after nine o'clock at night. This is another reason I'm so glad the universe put Ang in my path.

As we've already mentioned, the reason Ang and I found each other in the first place was because of her book *Reality Fitness*, a nutrition and fitness guide inspired by her favourite (only) dad. It was a privilege to work on that book with her. Interspersed with our weekly training sessions were also monthly editorial meetings as we plugged our way through, chapter by chapter.

I never went on the *Reality Fitness* program officially, but in working with Angela on her book, I absorbed nutrition habits as if through osmosis. For example, I used to boast about drinking a litre of milk a day. *Milk is healthy. Check me out! Being so healthy.* What working on *Reality Fitness* brought to my attention was that there is still a caloric component to the beverage that makes it much different than water. Without making a hardline decision about it, I naturally started shifting to more H_2O, and milk started to sour in my fridge before I could get through the jug. In the same way, I started bringing snacks along with me for my evening teaching routes, and I started integrating more fresh vegetables into my diet. (Did you know you can eat vegetables at *breakfast*?)

The small changes to my eating habits put a new lens on everything I did. It brought a stability to my energy and to my mood that I can't say I've ever felt before. Having experienced how food choices directly affect the body and brain, I asked Angela what Paul and I could do nutritionally to further increase our chances of summiting a mountain. How could we better fuel our bodies to maximize the benefits of our training? Her advice to eat a protein and a carb before each workout, and to follow workouts with the same, became a crucial influence in how my body would eventually change. My muscle mass increased along with my metabolism, making me stronger and leaner – both beneficial for a mountain trek. By the time of my return to Canada from our trip, I would find I had dropped 25 lb and my pseudo-asthma, too.

Don't get me wrong. This book isn't about weight loss. While eating was a *contributing* factor, the workouts would be the *determining* factor to my success on the climb. But around the time I visited the naturopath, things had started to slacken.

Throughout the winter, I'd slowly stretched the inch Angela had given me in letting me off the hook for that missed workout, bit by bit. Consistency is key, and I was consistent. Consistently missing a workout every week, that is. Walks with Nyx were half as frequent as they should have been, and the ones we were taking were often half as long as they should have been. I can't even use the cold weather as an excuse, given that we had an unseasonably warm winter that year with several days above zero. I must insist that I wasn't being lazy. It's just that tasks like crafting wedding favours and arranging seating charts were taking priority.

Somehow Angela could tell that I wasn't following through. Lucky for me, this type of behaviour is not uncommon and is part of her job to curb. Once the wedding was done, she made it clear that it was time to step up my game. Just like with nutrition, it doesn't matter how you frame what you do or don't do. The day-to-day action is what adds up and what counts. If I was consistently coming up short, it would be more difficult for me to make it to the top.

5895
Beginner Workout Four

*5895 metres above sea level is where you'll find the summit
of Kilimanjaro, the highest point on the continent of Africa,
and the highest free-standing mountain in the world.*

Warm-up		
Stairs or treadmill walk	5–10 mins	Light to moderate pace
Series One: Repeat the series twice		
1. Goblet squats	20	Moderate weight
2. Back lunge with hop	12/side	
3. Low jacks	40	
Series Two: Repeat the series twice		
1. Lateral shuffles	1 min/side	
2. Calf raises	25/direction	Moderate weight
3. Single leg forward hops	10/side	
4. Glute bridge pulses	25	
5. Standing palms-in dumbbell press	12	Light weight
6. Lateral Raises	12	Light weight
Series Three: Repeat the series once		
1. Walking	30 mins	Moderate pace

Hiking at High Altitude

Altitude sickness. While "sickness" might sound in line with a stomach bug or a cold, altitude sickness is quite serious and one of the most dangerous aspects of climbing Kilimanjaro. The affliction is a result of low oxygen at elevations around 2500 metres above sea level or higher. (Remember: Kilimanjaro comes in at almost 6000 metres.) The higher you trek, the lower the air pressure, which makes it harder to breathe. This lack of oxygen can result in moderate to serious conditions if you do not slow down or immediately descend to a lower elevation to allow your body to acclimatize.

Altitude affects people differently. Fitness level, nutrition, age, weight – these have as much influence as your eye colour. For some, even elevations of 1500 metres can cause blurry vision or shortness of breath.

There are three degrees of altitude sickness.

1. Acute Mountain Sickness (AMS) results in a headache, nausea, fatigue, loss of appetite and inability to sleep. This condition is very common and can make some trekkers feel terrible while others will feel only a little discomfort. If you experience any AMS symptoms, consider them a warning to slow down; acclimate your body to prevent more serious conditions like the ones mentioned next.

2. High Altitude Pulmonary Oedema (HAPO/ HAPE) is the development of excess fluid in the lungs, causing breathlessness, even at rest. It can also cause a high fever and coughing attacks resulting in frothy sputum.

This chapter is a basic overview of altitude sickness. Discuss any high-altitude trek with both your regular health-care provider and a travel health-care provider before your ascent.

3. High Altitude Cerebral Oedema (HACO/ HACE) is the development of fluid on the brain. This condition causes confusion, imbalance, lack of motivation, agitated behaviour, drowsiness and loss of consciousness before death, if not treated immediately. Often, HAPO and HACO occur at the same time.

This information is not meant to scare you but rather to inform you of the signs and symptoms of the varying degrees of altitude sickness.

Preparing for Altitude

According to www.altitude.org, two things certain to increase the risk of altitude sickness are: ascending at a rate faster than 500 metres per day, and vigorous exercise above 2500 metres. The body requires about a week to adapt to an elevation of 5000 metres.

The more time your body has at high elevations, the better you will adapt. This is why many routes up the mountain include days for acclimatization (days where you'll still hike, but just up and down within a set elevation range).

Certain pharmaceuticals can help the body at high altitudes. Diamox (Acetazolamide) is one of the most common and is best used as a prophylactic measure to (hopefully, because there are no guarantees) stave off symptoms. Talk to both your doctor and a travel health-care provider about your options.

Guides, Pulse Oximeters and Oxygen Tanks

Reputable trekking companies employ guides who are trained to spot the symptoms of AMS, HAPO and HACO. They will check in with you frequently and should travel with a pulse oximeter (a device that is clipped onto the tip of your finger and capable of measuring your pulse and oxygen levels), but you might consider bringing your own so you can monitor your levels more frequently. Reputable tour guides also travel with an oxygen tank when accompanying hikers up to high altitudes. While oxygen can help a person suffering from forms of altitude sickness, the only safe response to HAPO or HACO is to get down to a lower elevation as quickly as possible.

Again, there is no guarantee against altitude sickness, nor of a successful summit. If you feel any signs of serious altitude sickness while on a climb, inform your guide immediately and head down to a lower elevation.

Many sought-after peaks are within the elevation that puts humans at risk for altitude sickness. As mentioned, being physically fit does not protect you. Even Olympic athletes can be affected. Of course, every day in the mountains is an adventure, and no summit is ever a guarantee. Altitude sickness is only one of several variables you can't control. However, there are two variables that you can control. Give yourself ample time to train and prepare, and take your time hiking each day you are on the mountain. Going *polepole* is about more than conserving your energy. It's also about allowing your body the time to acclimatize so that you are much more likely to reach the summit (not to mention allowing yourself time to really take in all the sights along the way).

WE CAN ALWAYS JUST STOP IF WE NEED TO.

It was late winter when my feet got real cold. Post-wedding, at this point, and Paul and I had yet to book our trip. Travel books about Tanzania and Kilimanjaro were piled on the side table in our living room. With the Oilers game on in the background, Paul browsed the guides, evaluating the different routes we could take. I browsed the web, perusing blogs and YouTube videos about people's experiences.

In one clip, a young woman with dark hair and thick mascara swings the camera around from her teary-eyed face and scans the landscape ahead of her while describing how far up and down and up again she still has left to climb that day. The video ends in sniffles and sobs. Later, I came across a blog by a woman whose altitude sickness left her with migraines and puking on the trail. She writes about Barranco's terrifying "Kissing Rock" – an area on the trek where you risk falling backward down a rocky cliff side if you lean too far back.

When the hockey game finished, I took my huffy husband (the Oilers lost) and Nyx out for our requisite walk. While our commitment to the walks varied from day to day, we now respected the distances we had to put in every week, regardless of the temperature or of how late it would put us to bed. Cold and exhaustion would be elements to contend with on Kilimanjaro. Might as well get used to them.

That night we walked farther than usual, mostly in silence. *Is this whole idea even a good one?* I wondered. *People die every year on the mountain. Is that really a risk we want to start our marriage with?* My boots stamping fresh prints in the snow, I tripped down a statistical rabbit hole. If an average of five out of 35,000 people die every year on the mountain, that's... well, I guess it's still way less than even one per cent of trekkers. But still. That percentage is higher than the likelihood of getting struck by lightning. Or eaten by a shark! Frankly, even if we weren't going to die, the women whose stories I'd just read did not seem to be having that much fun. And if it wasn't going to be fun, then what was the point?

Breaking the rhythm of crunching snow, Paul.

"We should probably book the trip soon, hey? I'm thinking we should go with Lemosho. It's longer and will give us more time to acclimatize."

...

"What do you think?" Paul prompted when I failed to answer.

"I think I'm nervous. I'm worried about the risks."

I told him about everything I'd seen and read that night online, and it snowballed as I listed all the potential hazards we would be exposing ourselves to. Paul responded by doing what he does best.

A man whose spirit naturally embodies *polepole*, Paul rarely rushes, neither in action nor speech (unless he's on the ice). On our first date I noticed how he spoke...slowly...with a lot...of space. I thought it might have been nerves, but it's something that's never changed. Some might categorize this as a flaw, but I've always seen it for what it is: evidence of attention and intention. It has the effect of slowing my own pace down, of bringing my inclination toward frazzled to the point of at least being capable of thinking in a single direction at a time. It's why I married him. (That, and the idea of a live-in massage therapist was super appealing.)

That night, his effect was no different. As we walked through the midnight air, Paul broke the situation down to its simplest reality. He understood my concerns, and they were valid. But Kilimanjaro was a huge opportunity in our lives that we shouldn't turn down.

"We can always just stop if we need to. We don't have to go all the way to the top," he said.

"But what if I can't handle the altitude? Like. I would want you to continue. I think? But what if you have to stay back because of me? Will you still love me?" The question was half joke, half honest concern. What if in holding him back I introduced a seed of resentment to our relationship? One that would germinate a decade later, *leaving me alone and broken-heart –*

"Well," Paul halted my runaway thoughts. "That in particular would likely be a game-time decision. Either way. My love for you won't change."

I looked up to the stars and sighed, my breath visible against the glow of the street lamps.

"Yes. You're right. Okay."

"And maybe...it would be better –"
"If I stopped reading blog posts?"
"Yeah," he said.
"Yeah," I agreed.

By the time we kicked the snow off our boots on our front steps we'd decided on the eight-day Lemosho route with a trekking company we chose based on, among other things, its commitment to fair payment and good treatment of mountain guides and porters. The next day Paul filled out the online forms to reserve our spots on a climb in early August. Meanwhile, I handled flights via our travel agent. That settled, we made an appointment at a travel clinic where we'd eventually get all the prescriptions we'd need, including antimalarials, Ciprofloxacin (a catch-all antibiotic commonly prescribed to travellers who could fall victim to traveller's diarrhea) and Diamox, which we both decided we'd take for the entire trek to minimize our chances of altitude sickness. There was no guarantee this would make a difference, but there was no harm in adding it to the arsenal. We also got the necessary immunizations and (bonus!) a tetanus booster for me, after which I passed out into Paul's arms.

Back at our vehicle after the appointment, I breathed slow and deep, exhaling loudly as I buckled into the passenger seat. *Looks like we're doing it.*

"We can always just stop if we need to. We don't have to go all the way to the top," Paul had said.

What he wouldn't understand until we actually got there was that quitting while on the mountain is easier said than done.

INTERMEDIATE TRAINING PHASE

If you have just completed the beginner workout level and are now transitioning to the intermediate level, congratulations! If you are beginning your training at this intermediate level, welcome! The next six months will be a fun challenge, physically and mentally.

This set of workouts builds on the beginner phase. The exercises become a little more complex, and the muscular endurance demands increase. The length of the workouts is also more demanding of your time and mental focus.

Things You've Missed if You're Starting Here

Note on Nutrition (page 29)
Note on Altitude Sickness (page 36)

Equipment Required

- A foam roller
- A variety of dumbbells ranging in weight
- An exercise ball
- A mini-band (medium–heavy weight)
- Two small towels

Since these workouts are not tailored to you specifically, it is important that you listen to your body and place yourself in the appropriate training category. If after two weeks you are finding the intermediate workouts too challenging (you are unable to perform the exercises with correct technique), continue with the beginner workouts for a little while longer. Alternatively, if the intermediate workouts are not challenging enough, jump forward to the advanced workouts. Regardless, continue with the intermediate walking routine to build up your leg endurance. It is best to ease yourself in for as long as you can, especially since your hiking boots and backpacks will come into play later, as well.

A combination of the workout programs (beginner, intermediate and advanced) is absolutely okay and even encouraged since every individual has their own starting point.

Stair Sessions

Once the snow had melted for good, I added stair sessions to Erinne and Paul's training program. Climbing up and down a large staircase (over 100 steps is ideal) is a fantastic way to train since Kilimanjaro is basically an outdoor StairMaster. The mountain trek equals about 2,500 flights of stairs.

I did not incorporate stair training into the

Polepole program officially since many people do not have access to a long staircase or a StairMaster. As with most of my clients, Erinne and Paul's training was focussed on workouts like the ones outlined in this book and long walks with and without their boots and backpacks on. So, if you do not have access to stairs, not to worry. You will still be amply prepared.

If, however, you do have access to a long staircase or a StairMaster, and you would like to add stairs to your training, take the amount of walk time in your program and cut it by half for time spent on the stairs. (Stair climbing is more intense and therefore requires less time.) You could also do a split. For example, if you are required to walk for two hours, you could walk for an hour and then do 30 minutes of stairs. This helps save a bit of time and provides variety.

If you don't have access to a staircase, a long hill with a decent grade (one that makes you winded as you walk it) can serve as an alternative. Walk up and down the hill for half the allocated time of your walk that day.

If you don't mind being on a piece of equipment at the gym or at home, you can use a StairMaster or treadmill at an incline (between 10–15 incline) for half the allocated time of your walk that day.

The main objective is to be on your feet consistently, allowing your body to adjust to ever-increasing training times and intensity week-to-week, month-to-month. It doesn't matter if you are doing the stairs, climbing a steep hill, walking on a treadmill or walking outside – it is not necessary to go fast. A comfortable pace is key. The intensity piece comes into play during your workouts! (I'm not letting you off the hook completely.)

Where to Find a 100+ Staircase
- Stadiums or arenas
- Outdoor staircases in parks
- Green spaces traversing hills/cliffs
- Apartment buildings
- Professional buildings
- Universities

Kilimanjaro Trails
Each workout in this set is named according to one of the several trails you can choose to take up Kilimanjaro.

Workout Index

Intermediate Training Schedule (6–9 Months)

Week	Monday	Tuesday	Wednesday	Thursday	Friday	Saturday	Sunday
1	OFF	Machame	OFF	Umbwe	45-min walk	Marangu	90-min walk
2	OFF	Machame	OFF	Umbwe	45-min walk	Marangu	90-min walk
3	OFF	Machame	OFF	Umbwe	45-min walk	Marangu	90-min walk
4	OFF	Machame	OFF	Umbwe	45-min walk	Marangu	120-min walk
5	OFF	Machame	OFF	Umbwe	45-min walk	Marangu	90-min walk
6	OFF	Machame	OFF	Umbwe	45-min walk	Marangu	90-min walk
7	OFF	Shira	OFF	Rongai	45-min walk	Lemosho	90-min walk
8	OFF	Shira	OFF	Rongai	45-min walk	Lemosho	120-min walk
9	OFF	Shira	OFF	Rongai	45-min walk	Lemosho	90-min walk
10	OFF	Shira	OFF	Rongai	45-min walk	Lemosho	90-min walk
11	OFF	Shira	OFF	Rongai	45-min walk	Lemosho	90-min walk
12	OFF	Shira	OFF	Rongai	45-min walk	Lemosho	120-min walk

Intermediate Training Warm-Up Summary

All your workouts should start with a warm-up, which transitions your body from a cold, static state to a warm, mobile state while gently raising your heart rate. There are two parts to the intermediate warm-up.

1. Foam Roller Series

Foam roll the following muscle groups for 30 seconds each. Full descriptions available in Appendix A (page 285).

- Quadriceps
- Glutes
- Iliotibial (IT) band
- Gastrocnemius and soleus
- Latissimus dorsi
- Deltoids and latissimus dorsi
- Erector spinae

2. Treadmill Incline Walk

Walk on the treadmill at an incline of 10–15 (or outside if a treadmill is not available) for the length of time allocated in the workout summary. Go at a pace that allows you to carry on a conversation with someone but leaves you slightly out of breath. Your heart rate should increase slightly, and you may begin to sweat a little bit. It is okay to lean slightly forward at the hips while walking at an incline, but avoid bending too far forward. If you are unable to stay upright or must hang on to the treadmill to maintain your pace, decrease the speed of the treadmill to keep an upright walking posture.

MACHAME
Intermediate Workout One

Machame is a Bantu language spoken in parts of Tanzania. It is also the name of one of the most popular hiking routes to the summit of Kilimanjaro.

Warm-up		
Foam roller	See Appendix A	
Treadmill incline walk	5–10 mins	Moderate pace
Series One: Repeat the series three times		
1. Goblet squats	20	Moderate weight
2. Jump squats	15	
3. Calf raises	25/direction	Moderate weight
4. Mini-band lateral walk	12/side	Medium to heavy weight band
Series Two: Repeat the series three times		
1. Low jacks	40	
2. Sliding towel hillclimbers	30 secs	
3. Back lunge with knee tuck	12/side	Moderate weight
Series Three: Repeat the series three times		
1. Bench press off floor	15	Moderate weight
2. Walkout with push-up	8	

I MIGHT HAVE HAD ONE MORE ROUND IN ME. (DEFINITELY NOT TEN.)

Spring. The last piles of muddy snow melted and poured into city drains, making our neighbourhood streets sound more like creeks. On our monthly calendar, a new addition to the workouts and walks: stairs. It was midday, midweek, and Paul was at work. I, on the other hand, was looking for a way to procrastinate. *Why not give 'em a go right now?* Being close to the River Valley, I had several staircases at my disposal. I laced up my sneakers and set off on the twenty-minute walk from our home, past Whyte Avenue and across the High Level Bridge, to a popular set of stairs just south of downtown Edmonton.

Staring down the planks from above, the staircase didn't seem so bad. Paul and I had been working out for several months, now, and after a pep talk with Ang my commitment to training renewed. Confident, I imagined I could probably get up and down a handful of times, if not more, before breaking a sweat. *I'll probably max out somewhere around ten. Here we go.* I plunked my way toward the bottom. As I approached the ground, I heard a rumble from behind me and moved over to the side just in time as a stampede of young men from a university team trampled down and gathered at the base of the steps. Stair etiquette, they shuffled over and paused since I was technically first in line. Running in place, they waited for me to make my way back up. My heart dropped and I waved them ahead, pretending to answer a text on my phone. A string of young, buff dudes running up behind and then likely around me? No doubt smirking at my physical ineptitude compared to them? No thanks.

Accepting my surrender, they started jump squatting the steps two at a time. Then it was my turn. I shook off the discomfort and started jogging up. To my dismay, my body was not as primed as I thought. Barely a third of the way up, I waned from jog to slow climb. I considered stopping for a break on one of the landings, but the men from the team were already on their way back down past me, surely soon to be on their way back up again. My ego couldn't handle being lapped. Step by step by step, I pushed through the burn in my quads, reaching the top just as the team crested and curved back down again.

I might have had one more round in me. (Definitely not ten.) But I felt embarrassed and overwhelmed by the thought of being lapped over and over if I attempted to continue. *I've got work to do. I should probably get back.* Defeated, I started toward home. *What have I got myself into?* As I walked, head down in shame, I passed phrases sandblasted into the sidewalk – part of a high-school community initiative.

Dear unknown,

Bring it on!

I pulled out my phone to note the day and time so I could be sure to avoid the university team again.

After waiting a few days for my heart and legs to recover, I was back at the stairs, the glorious odour of mayflowers in the air. I gave myself a simple goal: two. Just do two rounds. And that's all I did. The next time: do three. And I did. Eventually I was hitting the stairs about two or three times a week, and Match or Beat was the name of my game. As long as I could at least meet my best, I could walk back across the bridge feeling content and accomplished. By the time the white petals of the mayflowers had confettied away, lilacs blooming in their place, I was at six rounds. As the trees bore berries, I made it to eight rounds.

The stairs was a simple routine, but it required discipline and will power to get in motion. When it was raining, I admit I didn't have enough of either to get me out the door. But when the weather was dry, I'd break from my work and load my backpack with a full bottle of water and the weightier books from my desk. In the sun, I'd slather my fair and freckled face in SPF 50 and think about the heat I'd need to get used to in Tanzania. Finally, earbuds in, I'd hit the tiny triangle on the Kili playlist on my phone and pumped myself up with songs by Janelle Monae, Rihanna, Sia, Beyoncé and Drake while taking each step *polepole*.

Indeed, I always took it slowly, slowly on the stairs. And when I decided I was on my last set for the day, I pushed my pace as hard as I could (though to the outside observer it probably looked no different than the pace I'd set from the start).

Paul came with me regularly, but my schedule allowed me to head out more often. No matter for him. He was always much faster and lapping me anyways. Sometimes I roped a friend into coming, but usually I went alone. Rarely was I the only one on the stairs, though. There was always a handful of other folks making their way up and down. Over the weeks I started to recognize familiar faces (or familiar leggings, to be more accurate). I imagined the conversations we could have. I was curious about their goals and wondered if they cared about mine.

What are you training for?

My husband and I are attempting Kilimanjaro this summer. You?

I was too shy to ever say anything, though, and reasoned that other people probably didn't want to be interrupted in their flow. So I went with the nod. More often than not, I'd get a nod back, and we wordlessly acknowledged and encouraged each other's efforts as we passed back and forth, back and forth. Back. And forth.

UMBWE
Intermediate Workout Two

*Umbwe is the name of the Kilimanjaro route that is considered
the most difficult due to its steep and direct approach to the
summit. Because of this, it is one of the least populated routes (and
of course the one Angela chose when she summited in 2007).*

Warm-up		
Foam roller	See Appendix A	
Treadmill incline walk	5–10 mins	Moderate pace
Series One: Repeat the series three times		
1. Squat with single arm press	12/side	Moderate weight
2. Single leg lunges	12/side	Moderate weight
3. Lateral lunges (dynamic)	12/side	Moderate weight
Series Two: Repeat the series three times		
1. Lawnmower	12/side	Moderate weight
2. Rear delt flys	12	Light weight
3. Plank off ball	45 secs	
Series Three: Repeat the series three times		
1. Glute bridge pulses	1 min	Moderate weight
2. Mini-band jacks	20	Medium to heavy weight band

THEN WE TOOK SOME TIME TO APPRECIATE THE VIEW.

After our first trip to Jasper National Park together back in September 2012, I was convinced that Paul and I were over.

Our first get-away had been picturesque. Post–Labour Day is usually a perfect time to visit Jasper because the weather is still pleasant and the kids are back at school. The environment made for an easy tumble into love. We'd spent the weekend soaking in the mountain vibes, cuddling in our cozy basement B&B at night and then emerging in the morning to spend the day exploring the park. Kayaking Maligne Lake, walking hand-in-hand around the cascading Athabasca Falls, revelling our meals and enjoying the coffee in the quaint town cafés. It was cliché and it was perfect. Until the drive home.

We'd planned a hike up the Sulphur Skyline Trail for our last day. September in Alberta can be either a late summer or an early fall (or, if we're really unlucky, a winter sneak-peek). That year summer was still going strong, the sun scorching. My heart rate was up already only a couple-hundred metres into the four-kilometre hike. Barely a third of the way into the trail, my head pulsed like a hammered thumb. Paul's shirt was soaked up the centre of his back, but he seemed to be doing fine. Clearly, I was out of my league, so I made silly excuses for breaks all the way up, taking an abnormal amount of interest in random rocks or trees. We summited several hours later and then hastily descended to the trailhead, hoping to squeeze in a dip at the Miette Hot Springs before hitting the road. We made it there just before it closed. In the hot springs, Paul proposed trying out a technique of going back and forth between the cold and hot pools. Something about it being good for blood flow. Polar dips are not my thing, but I didn't want to come off as a person opposed to new experiences. I was trying to impress! And so I did it.

Once.

Once was all it took. I plunged into a full-on migraine. Before we even got to the park's exit gates my head felt like it was slowly, relentlessly, being compressed in a vise. By the time we reached the next town to grab some painkillers from the grocery store, I was in tears. I stayed in tears – head hiding between my knees – the whole drive home. It remains, to this writing, the most pain that I have ever been in. Back in Edmonton late that night, Paul got me out of the car and into bed. He left only after I insisted that I would be okay, that my roommate was there if I really needed help.

I couldn't even handle a simple hike, I lamented while the pain slowly started to subside. *Probably won't hear from him again.* But in the morning, I awoke to a text from him anxiously waiting to know how I was doing.

Fast-forward to May 2015. Paul is now my husband, and we are taking that same hike. It was our first mountain hike since our training had started with Angela. Frankly, it was a cakewalk. We were already halfway up before I realized we had yet to stop for a break. The whole hike took half the time it had three years prior, including with the added trudge

this time through the knee-deep snow still clinging to the last pitch. At the top, we posed for strangers we'd entrusted with our camera. Then we took some time to appreciate the view, a never-ending expanse of green and grey. From this vantage you can pinpoint patterns in the rock. Other ranges look like their back halves have been folded in flat.

I looked down to the rocks around my boots and tried to imagine the time when they were sediments on an ocean floor. Turning my attention back to the mountains in the skyline, I followed the curves of their bodies and searched for faces in their peaks. I thought of all the human eyes over thousands of years that had traced these same features. I've always felt a spiritual connection in the Rockies, less to any particular deity than to the land itself. The mountains are my church, and I am not the first one, nor will I be the last, to think so. I am humbled by the mountains every time I go. When life gets chaotic (or in the times when it hasn't, really, but still feels

that way), the mountains ground me. Mountains are evidence of a story that has existed and will continue to exist beyond human existence.

Shit. I get real deep when I get to the top still able to breathe, I laughed.

"Cold pool?" Paul suggested as we reprised our Miette Hot Springs soak.

"No way. I've already got the ring. No need to impress you anymore. But you go ahead."

Elbows perched on the edge of the pool deck, I watched Paul across the way dunking himself into the icy water. I felt pride as I realized just how much *physical* progress I'd made in all these months of training. That progress had left me with space to benefit from the more spiritual aspects of mountain hiking. I felt excited for whatever lessons Kilimanjaro would have for me. For the first time, I felt assured. Would I be able to handle Kilimanjaro? *Totally.*

MARANGU
Intermediate Workout Three

*Marangu means "a place with too many streams." It is also
the name of another popular hiking route on Kilimanjaro.
Known at the Coca Cola route, it is the only trail where
hikers sleep in dorm-style huts instead of tents.*

Warm-up		
Foam roller	See Appendix A	
Treadmill incline walk	10 mins	Incline 15, moderate pace
Series One: Repeat the series four times		
1. Squats	30 secs	Moderate weight
2. Burpees	30 secs	
3. Single foot hops	30 secs/side	
4. Alternating back lunges	1 min	Moderate weight
5. Walkouts	30 secs	
6. Standing palms-in dumbbell press	30 secs	Light weight
7. Low jacks	30 secs	
8. Side-to-side jump lunges	30 secs	
9. Stairs	1 min	

YES, SOMEWHERE THERE WAS A BEAR.

With the success of our first practice hike, Angela suggested we take our workouts outside, which would start with a jog to a park nearby.

Running.

Outside.

My exercise nemesis.

I was nervous about the idea because it would reveal once and for all whether my "pseudo-asthma" was actually just "real asthma" and therefore something I'd need to accommodate on the climb.

Off we went, and not even halfway to the field I had to stop and walk. My ego sank as my chest heaved, lungs plunging my heart toward my stomach with every rapid, shallow breath. But while my heart rate spiked fast, it recovered just as quickly. And best of all – no wheezing! Bent over, hands grasping my knees as I caught my breath, I cheered with a roar.

"You alright there, Erinne?" Ang checked in.

"Yup." Breath. Breath. Breath. "Gonna be great."

Even though I wouldn't integrate running into any of my home workouts, jogging for a total of maybe ten minutes a week with Ang improved my stamina by the end of the month. Did I build better lung capacity within the short timespan (possibly), or did I simply learn how to pace my jog so that I wouldn't run out of gas before hitting the park? I can already hear Ang's response: "It's probably a mix of both, and both are important to the climb." (I guess she knows what she's doing.)

There were two spots near Ang's place that became our outdoor workout go-tos. The first was a field next to a children's playground. Between sprints across the soccer field and the usual body-weight exercises (squats and push-ups), Angela would toss the straps of her TRX up around a low goal post and we'd throw in...well, more variations of squats and push-ups. But this time at different angles! The second outdoor spot was a pond set centrally behind several backyards. Here we made use of a picnic table for...more push-ups at even more angles. Step-ups off picnic table benches were a common exercise, too, which just goes to show that you don't necessarily need a full staircase to get the same kind of leg workout. I was lucky to have access to both, and these two activities together built the cardiovascular stamina I would need for a week of uphill at higher and higher elevations.

I'll admit that I often felt self-conscious out there in the open. Kids riding in their wagons pointed at us, asking their caregivers what we were doing. With all the homes and their big windows facing the pond, there was always the possibility of prying eyes. *They're probably laughing at me.* But even this feeling I accepted as part of the training, a way to get used to being physically vulnerable while surrounded by strangers.

Every Friday morning that we knocked on Angela's front door felt premature, like we'd just seen her the day before. But it had always already been a full week. Kilimanjaro was a few months away, and then a couple of months away, and then just weeks away. I was feeling confident in my body but was still having reservations about all the things we couldn't control.

What if we fall off a cliff? My anxiety poked at me in the ribs.

Or get bitten by some poisonous bug?

Do they even have poisonous bugs on Kil –?

But what if?

I rolled my eyes at myself.

Paul and I planned a last trip to Jasper a week before our departure, picking out a few hikes to practise on. We wanted to break in our gear a bit more and, also, on the advice of our travel nurse, test how our bodies would respond to the Diamox while we were still on home turf.

We chose a hike called Valley of the Five Lakes to start our trip. A hilly walk, there's not a ton of elevation gain, so it would be a perfect warm-up. When we arrived at the trailhead, we were greeted by several other hikers making their way back out in a hurry. A duo with a baby peeking over her mom's shoulder in a fancy outdoor carrier warned us that there was a grizzly bumbling about in the meadows early into the trail. At that moment another couple who had just parked joined the conversation. It made sense that the folks with the kid would leave. It's hard to run with a baby on your back, I'm sure. But Paul and I had planned our itinerary purposefully and were not keen to change it. Yes, somewhere there was a bear. But in this park bears are like basement spiders – plentiful but elusive. The grizzly was probably already out of sight by now. We had our bells and our spray, so we decided to team up with the other couple, Niki and Greg, and started ahead on the path as more hikers left and chose another place to walk.

Turns out this grizzly was not so elusive. We were only about fifteen minutes into the hike when we saw it snacking away in the bushes along the opposite side of the first small lake. Still, with a body of water between us and the bear, we continued unfazed, confident in our numbers.

A couple of hours later we veered off the path to sit along the banks of another lake for lunch. Offering each other samples from our food, we got to know our fellow hikers. They were from Ontario and travelling the Rockies for the first time. They showed us pictures of their sweet camping trailer setup back at their campsite and raved about how amazing the Rockies are, reminding me yet again of how fortunate I am to live so close. Niki, a lover of elephants, was especially excited to hear about our plans for Africa.

The bugs becoming more persistent with each minute, we packed up our leftovers and trash. Time to move. We weren't far back into the hike when seemingly out of nowhere Paul called out, "Shit! There he is!" and darted up the path from the back of the pack. Paul didn't need to explain that "he" was the grizzly. For the briefest of moments my hands reached out, not for my spray but for my camera. Looking over my shoulder, I couldn't see him. A half-second later, common sense kicked in and all four of us hustled to put as much distance as possible between us and the bear, who thankfully wasn't in the mood for a chase. Admittedly, this was not the best way to handle a bear encounter. Ideally, you don't run.

Lucky for us, we got another chance to practise our wildlife awareness skills. At the end of the hike, a black bear off the trail by only a couple of metres essentially blocked our exit. Granted that a black bear is usually less intimidating than a grizzly, this time we didn't run, instead keeping a safe distance while waiting to see if he'd move farther off the trail into the bush. A few minutes later, he still hadn't budged. Unperturbed, he checked us out over his shoulder periodically as he munched away on whatever delicious grub he'd found. The energy in the air felt clear, but other hikers were starting to queue behind us, threatening to tip the balance. We agreed it was okay to go, so giving the bear a wide berth, we cautiously and respectfully made our way around and out.

Back at our vehicles, we exchanged full names and spellings with our hiking-mates so we could track each other down online and send "likes" back and forth while passively following each other's lives. I made a silent wish to the universe as we drove back into town. Our Kilimanjaro booking had space for a total of eight people, and I hoped they would be just as cool as Niki and Greg.

The rest of the hikes in our itinerary held lessons in weather. On Whistlers Mountain we crested the top just as a storm unexpectedly swung around the circumference of the peak, encasing us in thick cloud. We were stranded for over an hour at the top in the tram terminal with all the folks in tank tops who had come up via the gondola, which was down due to wind. On Edith Cavell we were caught off guard again, this time in a downpour that drenched us so fast that we didn't bother to pull out our rain pants. So much for testing out all our new gear before the climb.

As we drove back to Edmonton, I thought about our grizzly encounter, about all the ways the situation could have played out differently, for better or for worse. We knew the risk of the bear, and we went in anyway with barely another thought. Why was I so nervous about the risks of Kilimanjaro, then? Wildlife and weather pose hazards in the mountains on any continent. Here, sure enough, we came face-to-face with said risk. And we turned out fine. If I could feel confident walking onto a path where I knew there was a bear, could I not be just as confident for Kilimanjaro? Besides, the surprises we had managed on this trip were kinda part of the fun and made for a more interesting story.

Bent over in the passenger seat, I unhooked my laces. Pulled off my waterlogged boots and damp socks.

SHIRA
Intermediate Workout Four

*Shira, meaning "sail" in Swahili, is the name of the
route on Kilimanjaro that starts after your guides drive
you up to 3600 metres on the Shira Plateau, making it
more challenging if you require more time to acclimatize.
For this reason, the Shira route is rarely used.*

Warm-up		
Foam roller	See Appendix A	
Treadmill incline walk	5–10 mins	Incline 15, moderate pace
Series One: Repeat the series three times		
1. Squats with mini-band	25	Medium band
2. Toe touches	15/side	
3. Hamstring curls off ball	20	
Series Two: Repeat the series three times		
1. Single leg lateral raises	10/side	Light weight
2. Single leg forward hops	30 secs/side	
Series Three: Repeat the series three times		
1. Kneeling single arm shoulder press	12/side	Moderate weight
2. Alternating mid row	15/side	Moderate weight
3. Salamanders	15/side	
Series Four: Repeat the series twice		
1. Lateral shuffles	1 min/side	

Time to Start Packing!

What you need on a mountain trek depends on the length of your trip and the trekking company you've chosen to go with. While you *can* arrive and climb Kilimanjaro without a trekking company, you *cannot* climb alone. Current Tanzanian law requires that you climb with a minimum support crew of three people, even if you plan on carrying your own bags. Plan to bring one large hiking backpack that will hold most of your belongings (and that will be carried by a porter) and one small hiking daypack that you will carry for the entire climb. Chances are you'll have luggage for other excursions, as well, either before or after your Kilimanjaro climb. Most hotels in town at the base of the mountain (in either Moshi or Arusha) have locked storage specifically for this purpose.

Ensure you have, at minimum, the required items from the packing checklist provided by your tour provider. They will know what is being brought up by their team on your behalf and what they expect you to bring for yourself. One trekking company's packing list may differ from another's. Often larger items such as tents, sleeping pads, and cooking tools are provided and managed for you. Some other big items, such as sleeping bags and trekking poles, can be rented from your tour provider, though you might prefer to bring your own.

Confirm what is and isn't included/required with your trekking provider before leaving home. Depending on conditions, particularly at the summit, your tour provider might add additional equipment to the packing list at the last minute.

Packing List

Clothing and Hiking Gear

- 1 toque (a warm, knit hat, if you're unfamiliar with the Canadian term)
- 1 brimmed hat
- 1 pair of sunglasses
- 1 pair of warm gloves
- 1 pair of light gloves (optional, but handy to put inside warm gloves)
- 1 balaclava or scarf
- 1 down jacket or warm coat
- 1 sweater (one that zips all the way down is preferable for easy changing; fleece recommended)
- 1 long-sleeved base layer
- 1 T-shirt
- 1 set of upper and lower long underwear (thermal)
- 1 pair of socks per day of hiking (a mix of thin and thick socks is best for layering [the weather is highly changeable on Kilimanjaro] – a light pair for the lower parts of the mountain, and thick socks for summit day)
- 1 pair of underwear per day of hiking

- 1 pair of hiking pants (slightly big so you can add layers underneath)
- 1 pair of warm fleece pants
- 1 raincoat
- 1 pair of rain pants
- 1 pair of gators (effective against rain and dust)
- 1 pair of hiking boots (waterproof/ broken-in)
- 1 set of trekking poles
- 1 pair of sandals or light shoes (optional, for when you are at camp)
- 1 set of pyjamas (or use thermal underwear instead to pack light)
- 1 sleeping bag (rated −7°C minimum)
- 1 headlamp with extra batteries
- 1 two-litre water bottle
- 1 water bladder

You may want to pack extra shirts and pants if you like to feel a bit cleaner. Use your own comfort as a guide on how much you want to pack. Note that there are (rightfully) legal limits to the amount of weight porters can carry, so most reputable tour providers limit the weight each trekker can bring. Fully pack and weigh your bags before you go.

Toiletries
- Mosquito spray (the highest DEET percentage you can find)
- Sunscreen and lip balm (with SPF)
- Toothbrush, toothpaste, floss
- Toilet paper (at least two rolls – take the cardboard out so it takes up less space in your pack)
- Soap
- Feminine products, if necessary
- Small towel or sarong (these are light and dry fast)

Pack all your clothing in a dry bag or plastic bags. Your pack might be waterproof, but African rain has a way of getting in there anyway!

- *Optional:* Face and hand wipes, hand sanitizer, deodorant, nail brush and clippers, dry shampoo, a small sewing kit

Medications
- Any prescriptions you normally take
- Diamox (for altitude sickness)
- A prescription for antibiotics
- Antimalarial pills
- Nausea medication
- Painkillers (acetaminophen/ibuprofen)
- Bug-bite ointment and sunburn cream
- First-aid kit (your guide should have one, but have a small one with you just in case; fill it with Band-Aids, antiseptic wipes, pain killers, gauze, duct tape, etc.)

Nice-to-Haves
- Air pillow
- Pocket knife
- Phone
- Camera, video camera or GoPro (with extra memory and batteries)
- Music and headphones
- Small solar panel, charging equipment
- Watch with an alarm
- Book or eReader
- Journal and pen

Essentials

- Passport and driver's licence
- Yellow Fever card (for Tanzania)
- Credit cards (if you can, bring a couple of different varieties [VISA and MasterCard, for example] as not all places accept both)
- Cash (US dollars are widely accepted, but a little local currency is handy)
- Any other travel documents
- Emergency contact numbers and the number of your nearest consulate in Tanzania

Make copies of all your identification and travel documents. Keep a copy in each of your bags. Bringing a couple of extra passport photos can also save you a headache if you end up needing to replace a lost or stolen passport.

Day Packs

Remember that if a porter is carrying most of your stuff, he (or she – uncommon, but there are definitely female porters on the mountain) will be ahead of you. You will not have access to your belongings until you reach camp. Keep the following items in your day pack at all times.

- All "Essentials" (see list above)
- One full bottle of water and a water bladder (likely, your crew will fill these for you every morning)
- Water purification tablets or drops (in case you run out of water and must get more from a stream)
- Electrolyte replacement tabs or liquid
- Sunglasses, sunscreen and lip balm (at all times, even if it's cold)
- Mosquito spray (likely needed only on the first and last day of the hike)
- Layer of warm clothing
- Rain coat and pants (at all times; the weather can change quickly and dramatically, and you do not want to get wet at high altitude)
- The warm stuff: gloves, hat, scarf, balaclava, etc. (on the last day or two leading to the summit)
- 3–4 snacks (for energy, but also in case of an emergency)
- First-aid kit, medications
- Toilet paper and/or tissue
- Headlamp and headlamp batteries (in case of emergency)
- Small plastic bag for trash (Erinne's got a story about this one, too)
- Feminine products, if necessary
- The "Nice-to-Haves": music, headphones, phone, camera, batteries, memory cards, etc.

MY HUSBAND AND I ARE GOING TO ATTEMPT TO CLIMB KILIMANJARO.

Back home from Jasper, a handful of days left before our departure, Paul and I cleaned up our mostly broken-in gear and packed our bags. In the months leading up to the trip we had to buy a significant amount of clothing and gear – an expense we hadn't considered at the start – including waterproof coats and pants, fancy long underwear, several pairs of expensive wool socks, and proper hiking boots. Fortunately for us, our friend Mike worked for an outdoor outfitter and was incredibly generous in passing along a huge portion of his yearly discount allotment to us, saving us hundreds and hundreds of dollars. Between his discount, and items his brother Ben loaned us, we were able to cross off all the "required" items on our list.

We decided to do without certain "optional" items for the sake of saving a few bucks. Bad idea. Just get the gators. There were also some extras we opted to bring. For example, I decided our trekking company's suggestion of four pairs of underwear was decidedly not enough for an eight-day trek. Ten seemed a more reasonable number, and this is a choice I won't regret. When it came to snacks, we packed enough bars for three a day (though I ended up only eating three during the entire trek). I also brought eight portioned bags of gummy candies. Whether I like it or not, nothing gets my synapses firing like a wine gum. Finally, our Oilers jerseys. Paul had summited Fuji in his Oilers jersey with Ben and Mike a couple of years prior and was excited for another mountaintop photo-op to showcase his loyalty. Being the good hockey wife

I am, I obliged, folding and rolling the jerseys to protect their crests before stuffing them deep in the bottom of our packs with the rest of the summit gear.

The only items we left out of our packed bags were a full set of hiking clothes each, which we would wear on the plane. (I'd read several stories about people starting the trek without their gear due to delayed luggage, a porter sent up a day or two later to deliver it. Dressing in the majority of your clothes is highly recommended.)

Packing complete, I left our bags near the front door and retreated to our bedroom to relax and escape the July heat.

Sitting up in bed, I admired the new shape of my legs, running my fingers around my calves, past my knees and up over the hills that were now my quads. *Check me out! So muscly.* I'd never seen my legs like this, and I knew it was unlikely that I'd keep them forever. *Then again, if all it took was a few rounds of jump squats every few days, coupled with some time on the stairs...* While the truth is it took at lot more than a handful of squats here and there, the changes to my lifestyle had become habit, the effort had stopped registering as "work."

The day before, I had completed my last pre-Kili stair session. Finally, I'd hit ten rounds! I could've done at least one more, but I didn't want to risk heat stroke, and it was time to start conserving energy for the real thing. In just a few days, Paul and I would begin our attempt to summit Mount Kilimanjaro.

Attempt. This was the word I used whenever I spoke about the coming journey. "My husband and I are going to *attempt* to climb Kilimanjaro." This way, if my new legs didn't get me there, I would technically not have failed, because I had never said I was going all the way. Some might see this as a lack of confidence, others a sign of modesty. For me, it was just being realistic. There remained so many factors beyond our control. I'd be lying to say that I'd made peace with them, but even on my worst days I knew that at minimum we'd prepared our bodies to the best of our ability, all thanks to Angela. We'd seen her almost weekly for over nine months. Angela's expertise was why I could look down and marvel at legs I hardly recognized as my own.

At our last workout, to show our gratitude, I brought her a burned CD of tracks from my Kili stairs playlist (I know, old school, right?), a couple of homemade oatmeal cookies (one each for her and her husband) and a bouquet of bright orange gerbera daisies (my favourite flower, her favourite colour).

Angela hugged us and wished us luck.

"We'll try and keep your perfect record," Paul said.

"Don't even worry about that! But I'm pretty sure you guys got this. *Polepole!*"

We left knowing we had more than just our trainer rooting for us, we had a friend.

RONGAI
Intermediate Workout Five

Rongai is the only route that approaches Kilimanjaro from the north. It is generally less travelled than the other routes. It also has a more gradual ascent, making it a great option for hikers with less backpacking experience.

Warm-up		
Foam roller	See Appendix A	
Treadmill incline walk	5 mins	Incline 15, moderate pace
Series One: Repeat the series three times		
1. Front squats	20	Moderate weight
2. Alternating back lunges	12/side	Moderate weight
3. Glute bridge	1 min	Moderate weight
4. Calf raises	20 secs/direction	
Series Two: Repeat the series three times		
1. Alternating bench press	15/side	Moderate weight
2. Supermans	15	
3. Alternating mid row	15/side	Moderate weight
Series Three: Repeat the series three times		
1. Side plank off feet	30 secs/side	
2. Half burpees	15	
3. Plank off elbows	45 secs	

YOU WAIT UNTIL AFTER THE CLIMB
TO TRY TANZANIAN FOOD.

Paul and I landed at the Kilimanjaro International Airport in the afternoon on a Friday, a couple of days ahead of the climb. The trekking company's package included one night before the hike, but we requested an extra day to give us time to situate ourselves and get used to the time difference. After the lineups and bustle for visa applications and payments, we spotted a man wearing a blue company T-shirt and holding a sign with our names on it. His name was Hassan, and he was our driver. As we drove toward Moshi, past auburn dirt fields spotted with seemingly stray cattle, he taught us some of the important words we'd need to know in Swahili.

Jambo! Hi.

Asante. Thank you.

Asante sana. Thank you very much.

Karibou! Welcome.

I started to run my mouth like the excitable tourist that I am, explaining that "in Canada, where *we're* from, *Karibou* is an animal, similar probably to, I don't know, I guess an antelope?" Hassan listened politely and, when I stopped talking, continued with his lesson.

"Do you know *hakuna matata*?" he asked.

I took my eyes off the rickety shacks along the streets to look at his face in the rear-view mirror. Was he messing with us? Of course, I knew *hakuna matata*. (It means no worries. For the rest of your days.) Movies like *The Lion King* were integral to forming the romanticized vision of Africa that I

had in my head, but I'd purposely reminded myself before coming that Disney was not real life. Turns out they say *hakuna matata* in Tanzania all the time, though it's more commonly used in an "It's all good, no problem" kind of way.

Lesson over, Hassan asked if we had questions, and we cut to the chase: we would like to rent trekking poles, and my shoes had no insoles. Where was this shopping centre I'd googled? Hassan's response was not encouraging. It became clear at this point that the idea of an MEC in Moshi was naïve at best. "I will find you some. *Hakuna matata, hakuna matata*." Hassan left us at our hotel, and I realized he hadn't asked for my shoe size.

Our hotel was an off-white set of buildings, squared and gated, with a luscious central courtyard. Everything but the rooms was open-air, including the restaurant. Our room, called Kibo, was on the top floor and had a balcony that looked out back onto Moshi's streets, which were flooded with noise. Directly behind us was a Christian church, and beside that, the bus depot. Horns blared back and forth at each other like couples in arguments, no one backing down. Paul went to the railing facing back inside the hotel to connect to the Wi-Fi and checked the time as his phone calibrated to our new coordinates. The hotel restaurant wouldn't open for dinner for another couple of hours. Turning back to our room, we laughed at the two single beds.

"This is romantic," I said as we stretched out to relax for a bit, facing each other from underneath the mosquito screens, though we had yet to see any bugs.

When we woke up it was early the next morning. We'd slept through dinner, and then all night. I resisted the urge to joke about being able to eat a whole elephant for breakfast. Down in the restaurant, waiting for our omelettes, we eavesdropped on other tables where guests relayed stories about their respective summits in the days prior. There had been a lot of wind and snow. They'd all made it to the top but didn't get much of a view.

After breakfast we sat out on the walkway in front of our room. We were still getting our bearings and were nervous about getting lost beyond the confines of the hotel. Paul read while I took out my beading kit and started embroidering a flower I'd seen in the garden below to a loose square of velvet. The flower was small, with white petals that gradually changed to green by the time they reached the yellow centre. A teacher once told me that flower petals couldn't be green, that the colour should be reserved for leaves and stems. *I suppose she's never seen this flower befo* – "Oh hey!" Hassan suddenly appeared to my right. He had the trekking poles we'd requested and three pairs of used insoles from men's boots. Overjoyed and so grateful, I didn't bother to ask how he'd found them. Paul paid him for the insoles and tipped him for the favour. He had other tasks to complete this morning, Hassan said, but he would take us for a tour of Moshi later. While we waited for him to return, I examined the insoles carefully and picked the pair that seemed best, fully aware that they might have already been on the summit. Using the

tiny scissors in Paul's Swiss Army Knife, I cut them to fit. This was one of two times the tool would prove handy on this trip.

A short while later, we followed Hassan outside of the locked gates of our hotel. He walked us up to the roof of Kibo Tower. The highest building in town, it was either under construction or going through some extensive renovations. Ducking under plastic barriers in doorways, we left footprints in drywall dust on concrete floors. I checked in with my body after having climbed the stairs up ten storeys. Hassan's pace was definitely not *polepole*. I hoped my cheeks weren't already flushed from the exertion. Moshi and Edmonton are about the same elevation (890 and 645 metres, respectively), so I couldn't even blame the shortness of breath on the altitude. From the top of the tower, we took in the view of the town and the nearby coffee and sugar-cane plantations. We had to trust that the mountain was in the direction Hassan pointed because smoke and clouds obscured the view. This is not unusual, he said. *Moshi*, after all, means "smoke" in Swahili.

Back on the ground, we trailed Hassan up railway tracks to an abandoned station. Before the airport was built in the 1970s, this was where Kilimanjaro climbers disembarked. Off the tracks, we went to the market, and Hassan – managing messages and calls on two cell phones – strung us through a maze of vendors and piles of produce. Tiny green peppers, humungous avocados. While walking past a woman asleep on a mound of oranges we crossed paths with another couple of tourists following their guide. Looking up and through the stalls, I could spot several other small groups, all led by their respective guides, none following the same line through the market.

Eventually it was lunch, and Hassan brought us to a restaurant called Indoitaliano. Not exactly the local fare Paul and I were used to seeking out when travelling.

"What's your favourite restaurant that serves traditional food? Maybe we could go there?" I asked.

"You wait until after the climb to try Tanzanian food," he smiled as he walked away. "I'll be back in an hour."

We understood what he was getting at and stayed at his spot of choice. While we waited on the patio for our pizza, we watched as locals walked to and from the market, carrying on their heads everything from full baskets of goods to a single red Converse All Star shoe. The restaurant ended up unable to take our credit card and so we reluctantly paid cash, nursing our drinks until Hassan returned.

When he did, we started a search for contact lens solution (something I realized was missing in our bags back at the hotel). Not many people wear glasses in Moshi, never mind contact lenses, and this meant walking to what felt like all the pharmacies in town. While Hassan spoke to the pharmacists behind the counter at our third stop, a woman with grey eyes stood directly in front of me, staring into my face, though I doubt she could actually see me. This is where the most vulnerable people in Moshi waited, it seemed, hoping that someone coming through would offer to buy their medicine. Hassan intervened and respectfully spoke to the woman while guiding her to a nearby chair. "No solution here," he said as we walked back out to the streets.

Finally, at the sixth pharmacy, we lucked out and left with a nearly-expired travel-sized bottle of fluid. Again, we paid cash, and again we tipped Hassan generously after he dropped us off at our hotel on time for dinner. We apologized for all the extra errands he had to run. We'd obviously spent more time preparing our bodies than we had our bags. "*Hakuna matata*," he said, leaving us with instructions to meet downstairs the next day at five for the pre-climb briefing.

"We're probably going to need more cash, hey?" I said to Paul as we climbed the stairs up to our room.

LEMOSHO
Intermediate Workout Six

Lemosho is one of the newer routes on Kilimanjaro and is considered the most scenic with its panoramic vistas. It follows a similar route to Machame but begins farther west. Because this route is generally taken over a longer number of days, it is better for acclimatization and therefore has a high success rate.

Warm-up		
Foam roller	See Appendix A	
Treadmill incline walk	10 mins	Incline 15, moderate pace
Series One: Repeat the series four times		
1. Lateral shuffles	1 min/side	
2. Push-ups	30 secs	
3. Mini-band lateral walk	30 secs/side	Medium to heavy weight band
4. Goblet squats	30 secs	Moderate weight
5. Jump squats	30 secs	
6. Back lunge with knee tuck	30 secs/side	Moderate weight
7. Double stairs	1 min	
8. Single stairs	1 min	

I WONDERED WHAT PREDICTIONS THE REST OF THE TEAM MADE FOR US.

We had earplugs, but little cylinders of orange foam have nothing on the sounds of Sunday morning in Moshi. The townwide call to prayer from a nearby mosque at dawn was followed by the ambitious rooster next door, who crowed continually thereafter like snooze on an alarm. At six o'clock, the first songs of worship bellowed from the church behind us, and the raucous noise of commuters at the depot next door revved up. After an hour we decided it would be less exhausting to just stay awake than fight ourselves back to sleep. The prayers and worship and traffic – even the crowing – would last pretty much all day.

Having totalled up our remaining US dollars, Paul and I were indeed short what we'd need for porter tips at the end of the climb. Timidly, we left our hotel without a guide in search of a bank. It being Sunday, the bank was closed. Left with the ATMs out front, I picked one and put in my debit card. The machine ate it. Thankfully we still had a couple of credit cards, but the next machine didn't seem to want to dispense any cash, spitting my card back out. After several different ATMs outside several different banks, we finally found one willing to work with us, and we maxed out the transaction limit. All the cash was in Tanzanian shillings. Would it be enough? We did the conversions – shillings, to Canadian dollars, to US dollars – as more tourists in similar predicaments started to line up behind us. We'd be cutting it close, but we didn't want to hog all the cash by taking a second helping of what was available. Chances were we'd be able to stop somewhere the next morning on the way to Kili, we reasoned. We would be wrong.

With time to kill, we continued our walk around Moshi and eventually found ourselves on the patio of a popular tourist café. Kilimanjaro coffee was on our list of things to try. As the server set my iced coffee down on the table, I realized my error. In my mind, flashes of that travel vaccine commercial – a tropical yellow beverage set against an azure blue sea, ice cubes (presumably full of micro-organisms my body couldn't handle) ominously clinking into the glass.

"Maybe if you drink it fast enough...before the ice melts?" Paul suggested, always one to look for a way to make things work. With no time to waste in the heat, I pounded back the beverage and hoped for the best. It took minutes for my stomach to grumble. Maybe it was bacteria in the ice or (more likely) the shock to my body of a large, strong coffee downed in twenty seconds. I lasted through our meal, but we eventually made a hasty return to the safety (or rather, privacy) of our hotel. Perhaps the universe was helping us out, though. Remember how Hassan had left us the day before with instructions to meet downstairs at five o'clock for the pre-climb briefing? Well, everyone showed up at three. Thanks to my harebrained coffee choice and hurried need for a private toilet, we happened to be there when Hassan knocked on our hotel-room door looking for us.

Gathered on the couches around a coffee table in the courtyard was our team: three guides and four other climbers. Our assistant guides were Denis and Fabian. In the lead was James, who called himself Jamesy and ended most English nouns with either "y" or "o." We discovered this was common to many Tanzanians speaking English as a second (or third, or fifth) language, and I would get used to being called "Erinny" on the climb.

The moment felt like meeting cast members at the start of a reality TV show – part excited to get to know one another and part sizing each other up, inevitably making secret predictions. Who's most likely to make it with ease? My bet was on Roman, a man in his late twenties from Seattle, with light hair and eyes. He wore a large brimmed hat, his workplace logo on the back, a baseball logo on the front. He'd prepared using one of those breathing apparatus bags that mimic lower air pressures. Short term, he planned to summit Kilimanjaro and take a picture at the top with a bottle of the energy drink his company represented. Long term, he planned to complete the seven summits. I appreciated his hustler attitude and that he planned to capitalize on his summit. *Dammit*, I thought. *We forgot Angela's towel with her logo! Or even a flag.*

Deborah was Roman's mother. She was also in business but lived overseas. She hadn't seen her son in a couple of years but was intrigued by his Kilimanjaro plans and decided to join him. Her short, dark hair reminded me of a cut I'd had years ago, and I could sense elements of myself in her. Ambitious, perhaps a bit audacious, and the type to see value in following whims. She wanted to spend time with her son, and this was where she would find him. Africa? Yes. Let's go.

Mike and Krista were next, a couple probably in their late twenties and also on their honeymoon (and one-year anniversary trip). Both creatives. Mike worked as a video editor on a popular comedy show and Krista as a visual manager, designing displays and window fronts for a big retail store. They lived in LA and had prepared by hiking in the Californian backcountry on their days off. "Both have several tattoos," I would write in my journal (though I didn't specify what or where they were and have now forgotten). This meant that obviously Mike and Krista were cool.

Relief! Everyone seemed nice, fit, and level-headed. I anticipated that we'd get along well. Paul and I introduced ourselves next, and I wondered what predictions the rest of the team made for us. Paul, his calmness paired with his tall and broad stature, likely seemed a sure-shot for the top. And then there was me. At barely a couple of inches over five feet, scarf wrapped around my legs like a skirt and pencil holding up my hair, decidedly the most bookish of the bunch, I probably came off as a wildcard.

Introductions over, the meeting segued into reminders of what we'd read in the company documents and a check-up on equipment. Did everyone have a sleeping bag? Check. Did everyone have a rain coat? Check. Hiking boots? Check. Water bladder? Che– Deborah stopped him, pulling out a single water bottle from her purse. "Will this be okay?" James paused and slowly his pen crossed the premature check into an X on his paper. Had she misunderstood the list and thought the water bladder was one of the optional items? If this were a reality show, Deborah just made herself out to be the underdog. Finding his breath, James: "*Hakuna matata*. We'll find you a camel pack-y."

Back in our room after the meeting, Paul and I unpacked and repacked our bags one last time to make sure we had everything. In doing so, I found the missing bottle of contact lens solution. We decided to not tell Hassan about this.

My stomach was still rolling. At this point, though, it had less to do with the coffee and more to do with anxiety as the hours before the climb became fewer and fewer. I'm not usually one for prayer, but with the worship (still) radiating from the church behind us I thought, *why not*, and sent a request up for calmer nerves and calmer bowels.

ADVANCED TRAINING PHASE

If you have just completed the intermediate workout level and are now transitioning to the advanced level, congratulations! If you are beginning your training at this advanced level, welcome! The next three months will be a fun challenge, physically and mentally, with a variety of new workouts for you to add into your regular training routine.

This set of workouts demands even more from your cardiovascular system and muscular endurance than the previous two phases. The workouts will require more time and mental focus. Be prepared to sweat.

Since these workouts are not tailored to you specifically, it is important that you listen to your body and place yourself in the appropriate training category. If after two weeks you are finding the advanced workouts too challenging (you are unable to perform the exercises with correct technique), please move to the intermediate workouts for a little while longer, but maintain the walking distances at the advanced level. A combination of the workout programs (beginner, intermediate and advanced) is absolutely okay and even encouraged since every individual has their own starting point.

What You've Missed If You're Just Starting Here
Nutrition: page 29
Altitude Sickness: page 36
Stairs: page 41
Packing: page 55

Equipment Required
- A variety of dumbbells ranging in weight
- An exercise ball
- A mini-band (medium–heavy weight)
- Two small towels
- Skipping/jump rope
- Foam roller
- Your Kilimanjaro daypack and hiking boots

Workout Index

Tanzanian Culture

Each workout of this phase is named after a cultural element you are likely to encounter on your trip in Tanzania.

Advanced Training Schedule (3–6 Months)

Week	Monday	Tuesday	Wednesday	Thursday	Friday	Saturday	Sunday
1	OFF	Chagga	OFF	Maasai	Kitenge	45-min walk	90-min walk
2	OFF	Chagga	45-min walk	Maasai	Kitenge	45-min walk	90-min walk
3	OFF	Chagga	45-min walk	Maasai	Kitenge	Shuka	90-min walk
4	OFF	Chagga	45-min walk	Maasai	Kitenge	Shuka	120-min walk
5	OFF	Chagga	45-min walk	Maasai	Kitenge	Shuka	120-min walk
6	OFF	Chagga	45-min walk	Maasai	Kitenge	Shuka	150-min walk
7	OFF	Mbege	45-min walk	Chapati	Ugali	Acacia	150-min walk (B&B, no weight)
8	OFF	Mbege	45-min walk	Chapati	Ugali	Acacia	180-min walk (B&B, 10 lb)
9	OFF	Mbege	60-min walk	Chapati	Ugali	Acacia	180-min walk (B&B, 12 lb)
10	OFF	Mbege	60-min walk	Chapati	Ugali	Acacia	180-min walk (B&B, 12 lb)
11	OFF	Mbege	60-min walk	Chapati	Ugali	Acacia	180-min walk (B&B, 15 lb)
12	OFF	Mbege	60-min walk	Chapati	Ugali	Acacia	180-min walk (B&B, 20 lb)

Walking

In this phase, when you do your walks, be sure to wear your Kilimanjaro hiking boots and day pack to break them in. Add 10–20 lb (4.5–9 kg) of weight to your backpack to further train your legs, core and upper body. During longer walking sessions, it is okay to stop for short breaks periodically, but aim for no more than five to ten minutes per break.

Advanced Training Warm-Up Summary

All your workouts should start with a warm-up, which transitions your body from a cold, static state to a warm, mobile state while gently raising your heart rate. For this stage of training, there are two parts to the warm-up, and the walking portion includes a weighted pack.

1. Foam Roller Series

Foam roll the following muscle groups for 30 seconds each. Full descriptions available in Appendix A (page 285).

- Quadriceps
- Glutes
- Iliotibial band
- Gastrocnemius and soleus
- Latissimus dorsi
- Deltoids and latissimus dorsi
- Erector spinae

2. Treadmill Incline Walk

Carrying your Kilimanjaro daypack with weight, walk on the treadmill at a 10–15 incline (or outside if a treadmill is not available) for the length of time allocated in the workout summary. Go at a pace that allows you to carry on a conversation with someone but leaves you slightly out of breath. Your heart rate should increase slightly, and you may begin to sweat a little bit. It is okay to lean slightly forward at the hips while walking at an incline, but avoid bending too far forward. If you are unable to stay upright or must hang on to the treadmill to maintain your pace, decrease the speed of the treadmill to keep an upright walking posture.

CRISIS AVERTED, IT WAS TIME TO GET BACK TO THE BUSINESS OF TRAINING TO CLIMB A HUGE MOUNTAIN.

Because Erinne and Paul had plenty of time between their first workout and their trip to Tanzania, I went with a slow and steady approach to training them for Kilimanjaro. As I do with all clients, I considered their differing levels of fitness at the start, as well as their schedules. I knew the plan had to be manageable – in intensity and time – to keep them consistent and not overwhelmed, but challenging enough so they would build upon their fitness levels every week. In addition to our weekly training sessions, I had them completing a couple of workouts on their own and then simply walking more regularly with their dog to get used to being on their feet for longer periods of time.

At our Friday workouts, Erinne and Paul would report on their progress. Early on, they were very compliant with the training schedule I sent home with them each week. Not every single workout was completed, but most were. Erinne and Paul's wedding was set for the end of February, so they had a little extra motivation to look and feel their best for that special day. I ran with it and greedily used every bit of motivation they had to increase their training. It was also around this time that Erinne began slowly adopting some of the nutrition habits I had described in my book. As she was editing the content, it resonated and inspired her to dabble in some nutrition changes. I tried to play it cool so as not to create some kind of expectation

that she change her whole way of eating on top of the physical lifestyle changes she was already making, but when she mentioned little things like adding more vegetables into her meals, drinking more water and paying a bit more attention to how much processed food she was eating, I was elated!

Things started off strong, but then the temperature dropped and snow started to fall. With short daylight hours, and ice making walking conditions less than ideal, it's not unusual for Canadians' hibernation urges to impact motivation and keep them inside. Erinne and Paul were no exception. But weather wasn't an acceptable excuse for missing their *indoor* workouts. With the start of 2015, and their wedding fast approaching, routine was no longer routine, and other tasks started to take priority. They never specifically said this to me, but Erinne and Paul's weekly progress reports became less and less detailed. As a personal trainer, you know this is code for: "We didn't do what we were supposed to, and we don't want to make excuses. We will just gloss over the details, and hope you don't say anything and give us a chance to regroup."

I was comfortable with this because we still had a good amount of time to prepare. I considered the early months of training as bonus months to teach them the fundamentals of weight training and to set the tone for what the "real" training would be like going forward. In my mind, we were just getting started. By the time their wedding day arrived, Erinne had lost some weight and her body composition had changed. Her two gowns – one strapless and one backless and form-fitting – looked absolutely stunning! Paul looked exceptional that day, too. It was the first milestone in their training together, a great way to start their marriage. But once they were back home, it was time for them to start taking their training more seriously.

I knew how much work they still had to do in order to be ready because I'd been to Kilimanjaro, but to explain that to someone who has never been on a mountain that size is difficult. It's one of those things you simply can't understand until you've felt it. All you can do is prepare physically and mentally as much as possible so you have the strength and stamina to push when things get hard. Erinne and Paul's training grace period was over, and it was my job to tell them so.

During an early spring workout, I could see Erinne a little more flushed and out of breath than she would have been a few months back. Her questions were increasing and becoming more random again. She was trying to delay the next exercise. Likely, this session felt harder than intended because her workouts between our Friday sessions had been less consistent. Erinne's performance was noticeably less strong in comparison to Paul's, since he still played hockey on a regular basis throughout the week. Every little bit of exercise matters and adds up. I would need to talk with her later.

I looked over at Paul, who'd been doing well that day but whose head was now lowered and shoulders slouched. Was he okay? He was right in the middle of an intense metabolic series that was intended to challenge his cardiovascular endurance.

That's trainer talk for a series that's "really fucking hard." But he is not one to complain (ever), and it was not like him to appear so defeated in the middle of a workout. This type of training is right up his alley.

"You doing okay there, Paul?" I asked.

He didn't respond right away, but Paul tends to take time with his words. I waited with trepidation. Slowly, he lifted his head up and shook it side to side as sweat dripped from his eyelashes. "I'm okay. It's just that…I hate… Pink. So…much. So…much." He was referring to the artist singing on the radio. I burst into laughter, relieved and surprised all at the same time. My initial thought was: *Thank goodness he is okay!*

"All this time we've been listening to pop music and *now* you tell me you don't like it?" I said. "I would have happily played something you enjoyed." When I say Paul does not complain, I really mean it. Paul is one of the easiest going, relaxed people I've met. In his presence you immediately feel calm, never judged and at peace. It took months and one really tough interval leg workout to crack him! To this day, I make sure I never have Pink on the playlist. Instead I tuck "Dream No More" by Metallica into the mix. It's sometimes hard to believe that Paul can move faster, but when Metallica comes on, that Zen man turns into a beast!

After the workout that morning was complete, I had an opportunity to explain the urgency of the workouts at this stage to Erinne and Paul. Training motivation ebbs and flows for most people. Life happens, distractions take over, time gets away from us, routine is lost and motivation declines. This is normal and okay for a short period of time. But when you're training to reach the highest point on the continent of Africa, there had better be more training days than rest days. Their fitness levels still required improvement if they wanted a shot at a successful summit and a safe journey back down.

We were all on the same page: the days of missed workouts had to end. It was time to get back to the business of training to climb a huge mountain. With the weather warming and time ticking down, I suggested Erinne and Paul start incorporating some stair sessions into their weekly routines. Erinne had been having issues with her knees during some of the more traditional leg exercises. Walking up and down a large set of stairs in the River Valley would help increase her leg strength as well as her muscular endurance and cardiovascular fitness.

The stairs wound up being a key component to Erinne's success. After a couple of months of stair training (carrying a backpack full of books for extra weight), Erinne's knees were pain free and able to tolerate the lunges and step-ups that were a part of the necessary lower-body training. Her compliance with integrating stairs into her weekly fitness routine positively impacted her upper-body weight training compliance, too. This is very typical. As human beings, we are either all in or all out. If one area is going well, it often elevates another. Erinne was back on track, and it was just in time. Paul continued to play hockey, went to the gym and joined Erinne for several stair-training sessions. Of all the moments in our training, this was the one that gave me the biggest relief. I was feeling less anxious and more excited for them again.

With this success, they were ready to start taking advantage of being so close to mountain hikes

that would help even more with their training. Erinne and Paul decided to repeat the Sulphur Skyline trail they'd slogged up in 2012. It did not sound like that was an easy day from the stories they'd shared, but I was confident they would notice a huge improvement in their fitness level this time around. The moment I received the news that they'd made it safely up and down in nearly half the time, I knew they were ready for Kilimanjaro. We still had a couple of months of training to go, but the psychological impact of tackling that climb again with such ease would be a huge confidence boost and motivator. Once again, I took advantage of this and pushed harder during training. Oh, so greedy!

Summer in full swing, the three of us agreed that outdoor workouts would be a nice change of pace and good element training. Our workouts started with a short run to a nearby park and were cluttered with lunges, squats, step-ups, lateral shuffling, sprints and a few lower intensity "rest exercises." I did my best to keep the training varied, but the repetition was necessary in order to further develop their muscular endurance. There was never a complaint about it. These two knew that the climb was approaching, and they were dialled in with their training. I was feeling confident in their ability to make the summit, provided the altitude would not be a factor. This, of course, we could not train for. But the strength, muscular endurance and cardiovascular training was a success. They were ready – physically.

Mentally, the nerves were starting to set in a bit for Erinne. There are many unknowns in travelling to a foreign country. Hiring a guide you've never met, eating foods your stomach might not agree with, hiking at an altitude you've never been at, taking medications you've never taken before. You're uncertain of how your body will react, wondering if you'll enjoy the company of the other people in your tour group, deciding what you'll do if only one of you can continue to the summit, uncertain of the weather conditions. Paul didn't say much about it, though he might have felt the same way. All these concerns were legitimate, but there was nothing I could do to reassure Erinne. These elements were out of our control. But their *fitness* was in our control, and I would continue supporting her and Paul in their training to get them into the best shape of their lives so they would have the confidence in their bodies' ability to walk for multiple hours, uphill (and sometimes very steep), while struggling for breath in lighter air.

"I hate running. But at least I'll be trained for breathlessness on the mountain," Erinne would say every time we made the run to the park.

Comments like this reinforced just how mentally ready she really was.

Between the time that Erinne and Paul had their initial fitness assessment and the day they visited my studio for the last time before flying to Tanzania, a lot had changed fitness wise and personally for them. On top of now being officially married, they both had more muscle in their upper and lower bodies, stronger core muscles, better balance, improved cardiovascular systems and way more confidence in their chances of summiting. Paul and Erinne were conditioned to trek Mount Kilimanjaro. They had the right attitude, they had the lungs and the legs, they had a Kili playlist (with songs I'd mostly never heard of) and they had each other to lean on.

I tried to hold it together as Erinne and Paul packed up their workout gear for the last time before their departure. I was so proud of them and what they had accomplished together. It had been an incredible nine months of training with them. "*Polepole!*" I said as they left the studio. Slowly, slowly. Erinne and Paul would understand precisely what that meant in just a few days.

CHAGGA
Advanced Workout One

The Chagga are an Indigenous people, many of whom live on the slopes of Mount Kilimanjaro and Meru. They are the third largest ethnic group in Tanzania. Several porters and guides are Chagga, and so Kichagga is one of the languages you are likely hear on the mountain.

Warm-up		
Foam roller	See Appendix A	
Treadmill incline walk	10 mins	With backpack (10 lb) Incline 15, moderate pace
Series One: Repeat the series four times		
1. Front squats	20	Moderate weight
2. Glute bridge pulses	25	Moderate weight
3. Mini-band lateral walk	20 steps/side	Heavy weight band
Series Two: Repeat the series four times		
1. Jump squats	15	
2. Half burpees	15	
Series Three: Repeat the series three times		
1. Plank off ball with press-outs	1 min	
2. Push-ups with alternating rotations	8/side	
3. 3-point mid row	12/side	Moderate to heavy weight
4. Rear delt flys	15	Light to moderate weight

PORTERS PUT OUR BAGS INTO LARGE WATERPROOF SACS AND HURLED THEM UP ONTO THEIR SHOULDERS.

At 8:30 in the morning we were set to begin our trek, a long burgundy van pulled up in front of our hotel lobby. James weighed our bags on an old scale and then passed them off to a porter to load. Six seats in the vehicle were reserved for us climbers. The guides shared space up front, and the rest of the support crew crammed into the back third. Literally in each other's laps, they tapped messages on their old flip phones. After the quintessential bumpy ride on dirt roads consisting of more potholes than not, we arrived at the Londorossi Gate, where baggage was weighed again and we were signed-in to the park. Upward of a hundred men not affiliated with a company huddled in groups all around us, ready and waiting to be hired on the spot.

One of our guides handed each of us a square box. Lunch. Fried chicken, a huge burger topped with a fried egg, a banana and juice. The digestive issues from the day before had subsided, but in addition to the lunchbox containing just way too much food, my nerves still had a grip on my stomach. I ate what I could and passed the rest off to Paul, who is, in his own words, "always a little hungry."

As our bags were reloaded onto the top of the van, I took a quick trip to the bathroom. *This is my last chance pre-trek for a toilet,* I thought.

I locked the door and turned around.

No toilet.

In my head I thanked Angela for preparing me for this moment, for all the squats that now helped keep me from losing balance and toppling over into the puddles of piss encircling a hole in the cement floor.

Back in the van, things got a little tighter with the addition of one more porter, selected by James when our bags ended up weighing slightly more than the legal per-porter limit. Our newest recruit punched a message into his old Nokia. *Picked up a trek,* I imagined him typing to his brother at home. *Will be back in eight days.*

From the Londorossi Gate, we drove for another short while, passing fields of women wrapped in bold, patterned cloths, working in the crops of Kilimanjaro's lower slopes. At the Lemosho trailhead, we all unloaded once again. Porters put our bags into large waterproof sacs and hurled them up onto their shoulders where they landed perpendicularly across the top of their own packs. The combined gear a cross on their backs, the porters started up the trail in single file. Meanwhile, tourists took turns getting pictures at the wooden sign marking the start of the hike. A few family groups, their sons and daughters in shorts and sneakers, I assumed were here for a day-hike. The rest of us, despite coming from all areas of the globe, looked pretty homogenous in our hiking slacks. Our fleeces and moisture-wicking fabrics. Our trekking

fingers, stroking the delicate petals. I looked up to see Paul stopped several metres ahead on the path, looking back toward me, waiting.

"I'm coming, I'm coming!"

We arrived only a few hours later to MTI Mkubwa Camp, also known as Big Tree Camp. At about 2900 metres, I was already at the highest elevation I'd ever been. So far, I was feeling good. Several different trekking companies had clusters of tents set up with no obvious boundaries. James escorted us to our site where three identical orange tents were lined up side-by-side. Inside each were our bags and two sleeping mats covered in red and green plaid Shuka fabrics. Paul and I settled into our tent and re-emerged to an orange plastic tub with a few inches of warm water, meant for washing up. Before moving to the mess tent for dinner, we were called together to meet the porters. Nineteen men total, they were each introduced by their name and tasks. Some on the tent crew, making up and taking down our beds each day. Others on kitchen duty. Together they would provide us with three massive and nutritious meals every day. Finally, there was one unlucky fellow whose job was to set up and empty a private flush toilet for the six foreigners.

"Extra tips for that guy," said Paul quietly.

All the men, regardless of duty, would carry several pounds of gear up on their shoulders or heads for the duration of the trip. I would have a hard time remembering their names, most of them names I'd never heard before. But I could remember their different characteristics, and so I picked out unique traits while shaking each of their hands. The man with the goatee. The man with the skull on his toque. I would not take their efforts for granted.

poles extended and plugged into the earth by our feet as though we were charging up.

It felt like we stood around waiting for a long time until, unceremoniously, James moved toward the trees and we followed him into the rainforest. The first pitches were muddy and very steep. I braced myself for a long, long ride. But soon I was overtaken by the lushness of the greenery surrounding me. The path curved up and down and straight, but I took little notice of the varying degrees of difficulty throughout the walk. Everywhere: layers and even deeper layers of giant trees and leaves, bushes, vines. The only brown was the half-metre-wide path under foot. I stopped several times to admire the unusual flowers that lined the trail. Blooms that looked like miniature horns, florescent yellow and red. "*Impatiens kilimanjari*," our guide Denis told me. I held one gently between my

Introductions complete, we ducked into the mess tent for our first on-mountain meal. Six camp chairs were set up around a covered table, all the condiments you could imagine needing were pushed to one side, a steel pot of hot soup in the centre. We ate course after course of food – chicken, fried potatoes, oranges – our waiter Kijani checking in with each of us before taking any dishes away. "Are you all finished, Erinny?"

After dinner our guides came into the tent to review what we could expect for the next day before bidding us goodnight. "*Lala fofofo.*" Sleep soundly. There was a lot to digest that night – the bumpy ride to the national park, the chaotic energy at the entry gates, the realization that everything we'd worked up to had now officially started. I didn't sleep *fofofo*. I woke up several times to troupes of monkeys somewhere off in the distance, a chorus of hoots approaching closer and then passing off farther again as they coursed through the trees in the elevations beneath us. No, I didn't sleep *fofofo*, but I was *furaha*. Happy.

MAASAI
Advanced Workout Two

One of Africa's best-known peoples, the Maasai are semi-nomadic and live primarily in Kenya and northern Tanzania. They wear brightly coloured textiles and intricate, beaded jewellery. The Maasai work hard to maintain their culture, but don't be surprised when you see them in their traditional garb chatting away on cell phones.

Warm-up		
Foam roller	See Appendix A	
Treadmill incline walk	10 mins	With backpack (10 lb), Incline 15, moderate pace
Series One: Repeat the series four times		
1. Squat with diagonal press	10/side	Moderate weight
2. Single leg lunges	15/side	Moderate weight
3. Stairs	2 mins	
Series Two: Repeat the series four times		
1. Salamanders	15/side	
2. Skipping/jump rope	1 min	
3. Burpees	10	
Series Three: Repeat the series three times		
1. Oblique crunch off ball	12/side	
2. Pull/press	12/side	Light to moderate weight
3. Lawnmower	15/side	Moderate weight

IT'S THE COFFEE. I PROMISE.

The first morning on Kilimanjaro, I stretched my arms through the sticky, moist sleeves of my base layers. We'd thought to "dry" our clothes on a rope between two trees the night before. This was a mistake. If anything, they were now damper, and we realized that what works in the drier climates of Alberta or California does not work in the humidity of a rainforest.

Paul and I were last inside the mess tent where our teammates awaited us at a table yet again full of food. I settled on eggs and hot porridge, mixing in a scoop of chocolate hazelnut spread. (Yeah, that's right. Nutella in your porridge. You're welcome.) For a brief moment, I acknowledged and honoured the teenager in me who had spent hours eating oatmeal in front of the TV, dreaming of my future travel adventures. *Check me out! Eating oatmeal on Kilimanjaro.* I pulled out one of my Starbucks instant coffees and poured myself a mug of hot water. Another mistake. By the time James came into the tent for our morning health check, my heart rate was high. He eyed me nervously as he pulled the pulse oximeter off my pointer finger. I assured him that the altitude wasn't already starting to be a problem. "It's the coffee. I promise." As we left camp and started up the day's trail, I could feel my heart beating through my ribs. Reluctantly, I decided I'd need to opt for the less-potent instant Africafe provided from then on.

The second day's trek quickly brought us above the canopy and into the heath where the trees shrank and dispersed. There was much less green. And a lot more dust.

So much dust.

If I had to describe the day by a single sound, it would be that of porters expertly hawking and spitting to expel the dirt in their airways. I had a hard time picking up this skill and instead stopped frequently to blow my nose, trying not to examine the black streaks in the tissue for longer than socially appropriate.

There were several steep pitches paved with large stones that required a significant amount of lunging. I felt strong the whole time. Still, I remained at the back of the pack, our guide Fabian behind me to bookend our group, which was spread out over a hundred metres or so. Poor Fabian, stuck with me asking questions like a toddler. "What's that?" I pointed to a tree in the distance. "What's this?" I pointed to a bush just off the path. "What's that called?" I pointed to a strange...tree? Bush? Whatever it was (turned out to be lobelia), it looked like it came straight outta Dr. Seuss.

Halfway up another steep pitch, we rejoined the rest of the team taking a break.

"No, it's okay. You go ahead." Deborah was talking to Roman. "I'm fine, you go."

James said something to Fabian in Kichagga and then continued up the pitch, Roman reluctantly following behind him, and then Krista and Mike. Paul, who'd been maintaining a pace that allowed him to still see where I was, looked at me. "You go ahead, too. I'm gonna take a break," I said, catching his eyes. He knew what I was doing.

"No, no. You go ahead," Deborah said to me as Paul turned away and up. "Really, I'm okay."

"Do you have electrolyte tabs?" I asked her while grabbing a tube from my daypack.

"No, no. You need those."

"Nah, we brought lots of extra. Here."

I motioned for her water. She accepted, and I popped a couple of the small, iced-tea flavoured pucks into her bottle. It turned the liquid yellow and fizzed.

"What are you drinking? Beer?" Fabian joked.

"Haha, I wish."

Deborah moved slowly, but determinedly, for the rest of the day. Still, when it came to *polepole*, I had her beat, taking my time on the path and continuing to bug Fabian.

"What's that one called?"

Lunge, lunge, deep lunge.

Stop.

"What about this one?"

"No, I need to sit down for a bit. Everyone else already got a break."

I felt for Deborah. It'd become clear that she'd underestimated the physical nature of the climb. This isn't uncommon for Kilimanjaro – a mountain marketed as accessible, with summit stories from seven-year-olds to seniors. Individuals with missing limbs, people who are blind, groups of cancer survivors. And it's true! Anyone can do it. But those stories don't detail the preparation that likely came before the climb, to the detriment of people like Deborah, who therefore arrive unwittingly unprepared.

I recognized the feeling of that first hike with Paul – the same exasperation and dismay unmistakable in Deborah.

We were the last team to arrive to Shira Camp 1 on the plateau that day. Shira was one of the three volcanic cones on the mountain. Having collapsed half a million years ago, all that remained was a caldera around which tents were now spread out.

After the one and only video diary Paul and I would record on the mountain, I left the tent for some air. I was feeling a little light-headed at 3500 metres. After a quick visit to the toilet tent, I walked to a small embankment and sat cross-legged on a large rock facing Kibo. Watching a small cluster of clouds making its way around Uhuru Peak, I reflected on the language of mountain climbing.

Words I'd heard tossed around the different groups around camp made me uncomfortable. To *conquer* the mountain. The *assault* on the summit.

The tone of these common phrases felt disrespectful. Violent, even. I prefer a different vernacular. One that acknowledges the spirit of the mountain. One that comes with reverence, knowing that the mountain is the teacher and the climber, a student. I'd put in everything I had to prepare myself for a successful summit, but I wasn't looking to conquer the mountain. I was hoping to conquer parts of myself – fears, insecurities, lack of confidence – and was hoping that Kilimanjaro would help me to do that.

Breathing slow, I took a moment to thank Kilimanjaro for the journey thus far. Then I asked permission, for both Paul and me, to summit. And then, I had to pee. Again. An unfortunate side-effect of the Diamox.

I was making my way back toward camp when Deborah approached me.

"I'm thinking of quitting," she confided.

Gah, do we have to talk about this right now? I thought, eyeing the narrow black tent only a few paces away.

"Oh?" I said.

I wasn't surprised, and while I thought that probably she should quit (for her own well-being), I didn't want to be the one to say so, nor did I want to falsely encourage her into making an attempt that I didn't feel she was prepared for. I can't recall the exact script of what I did say, but I acknowledged that the journey would get harder from here, and that this was the last stop on the trek where you could make your way back by car via a nearby park gate.

"You've got some time to think about it, though.

See how your body recovers overnight. Maybe talk to Roman about it?"

She went in the direction of the tent she shared with her son.

In the middle of the night I woke up to a familiar sensation, a tingling in my lower body. *Sigh.* I weighed my options:

A) Fight off the feeling and try to get back to sleep, inevitably getting woken up again.

B) Bite the bullet. Get up, go pee, and then fall asleep easily.

The latter equated to more sleep in the end, so I shuffled out of my sleeping bag, pulled on my camp shoes, strapped on my headlamp, unzipped the tent, unzipped the vestibule and rolled my body up to standing outside. I nearly fell backward as I looked up at the sky: a firmament crowded with stars. If Africa is the cradle of humankind, and the stars our ancestors, it makes sense that there seemed to be so many more of them out here than anywhere else I'd ever been.

This alone is worth it. If for some reason I had to quit, I could leave happy and satisfied by the trip.

But I still really, really, really want to make it to the top, I pleaded to Kibo.

Pretty please.

KITENGE
Advanced Workout Three

Kitenge is a fabric often worn by women in eastern, western and southern Africa. Multipurpose and often brightly coloured, kitenge cloth can be wrapped around the chest or waist to serve as a dress or skirt, over the head as a headscarf, or over the back and shoulders as a baby sling.

Warm-up		
Foam roller and dynamic	See Appendix A	
Treadmill incline walk	10 mins	With backpack (10 lb), Incline 15, moderate pace
Series One: Repeat the series four times		
1. Squat with double press	15	Moderate weight
2. Back lunge with forward kick	12/side	Moderate weight
3. Glute bridge	1 min	Moderate weight
Series Two: Repeat the series four times		
1. Push-ups off elevated surface	10	
2. V-Press	12	Moderate weight
3. Single leg lateral raises	12	Light to moderate weight
Series Three: Repeat the series three times		
1. Side plank off feet	45 secs/side	
2. Sliding towel pike	15	
3. Plank off ball	45 secs	

ERINNE, PUSHING POLEPOLE
TO THE EXTREME!

At the start of the third day, my head had mostly cleared and I was able to provide an improved report to James at the breakfast health check. I felt mostly proud that after the intense day before of uphill lunges, my legs felt no different than they had all week. As we collected our filled water bladders and sunscreened up our exposed parts, Deborah said goodbye, having decided to call it a trek. Denis, as the least senior guide on the climb, was tasked with accompanying her to the park gate an hour away where a vehicle was waiting to take her back to town, along with other people who'd also chosen to call it.

Deborah wished us all luck and went left, the rest of us went right and fell into our predictable lineup. Roman up front, Mike and Krista in between, and Paul a hundred metres or so ahead of me as I trailed behind asking questions about plants to James, who must've drawn the short straw that morning to end up at the back.

As we walked, I wondered if I'd done the wrong thing in quasi-suggesting that Deborah stop. After one particularly steep pitch early on, we passed out of the heathers to the somewhat level ground of the moorlands. But while the elevation gain was gradual, the distance was long – nearly eleven kilometres.

There were few plants in the area to ask about, and so I turned my attention to James, asking about his family back home. He answered politely but didn't return any of my questions. I caught him reaching his neck out to see if he could spot Fabian at the head of our line.

"I'm sorry," I eventually said. "I know I go real slow."

"*Hakuna matata.* You're doing it right, Erinny. *Polepole.*"

And so I shut up for a while. Despite a seemingly stark landscape, and hours both behind and ahead of me, I didn't find myself bored and reaching for my earbuds. Instead I entered a zone many walkers and hikers can relate to. I wouldn't consider it a meditation, exactly, but as I walked and looked and walked and looked, I thought of nothing else but what was around me. It was so refreshing to not be spending every spare mental moment making plans and backup plans, or strategizing how to maximize the productivity of my hours. There was only a single item on my to-do list. Walk. It was a special kind of euphoria – a replenishment. I was consciously grateful for it.

Our team clumped back together for a break near what seemed to be a man-made rock garden – several cairns left presumably one after the other as people passed by, the inuksuks left (presumably) by other Canadians. I resisted the urge to add one to the gallery. The break was over, and everyone quickly spreading out again. This is how we spent the day, our team moving forward like a worm: shrinking together for breaks at semi-prominent landmarks, stretching out over the distances in between. Shrink. Stretch.

Somewhere in the afternoon we realized we'd split off from the larger herd of trekkers toward a less-populated camp. Moir Hut was nearly empty, and there was no official checkpoint book to sign. Between us and only a couple of other groups, it felt as though we were the only people on the mountain, when any drone's eye view would prove there were hundreds of other trekkers making their way along different paths and stages of the hike simultaneously.

As I walked toward our tent, Mike emerged from his.

"Erinne, pushing *polepole* to the extreme!"

"You know it!"

It was only after I settled into our tent that I checked in with my body to discover that I had a headache coming in strong and fast, and that I felt a little short of breath. Paul handed me a couple of ibuprofens, which I took with a few heavy pulls of what was left in my water bladder.

A short while later, it was time to move again. Fabian brought us out for an acclimatization hike up

an area called Lent Hills. I kept my eyes on my feet to avoid the motion sickness I felt when I looked at the frame ahead of me see-sawing from side to side. Paul stood behind me and carried my water. Several porters were already there when we arrived, having made the extra trip because the top was a good spot for reception. I tried to steady my head by imagining who they were talking to on their phones. One was calling his wife, maybe, who put the phone to her baby's ear so she could hear her father's voice. Another calling maybe his mother to let her know that he was doing okay on his first stint as a porter, the other men were treating him well, and yes, he was eating okay.

My musings were not working, so I moved away from everyone and found a perch. I had no red-flag symptoms of HACO or HAPO, but I worried about the long-term outlook. *What if I'm just one of those people who can't handle altitude?* If I felt this way at over 4000 metres, how would I feel at well over 5000? The only thing I could do was breathe, and so that's what I did, falling into

an even breath pattern I'd learned many years ago during one of my yoga kicks. *Sama vritti*. My magic number was eight. Eight seconds in, eight seconds out. Since starting to work out almost a year prior, I'd only gone to a single yoga class. I found the spiritual nature of the practice too opposite the very physical focus of the work with Angela, and I didn't go back. Yet the knowledge of breathing – *pranayama* – I could still connect to. Eight seconds in, eight seconds out. I also had another trick up my sleeve, literally. I'd brought some mint and lavender essential oils on the trek, the idea being that I could use a drop or two under my nose to make visits to the outhouses that appeared sporadically along the trails a little less revolting. It was a good idea and worked well. But that day I opted to rub a few drops of each between my wrists. Bringing my hands up to my face, I breathed in the scent. Eight seconds in. Eight seconds out. I don't know how long I did this for, but the team waited patiently for me to finish. When I opened my eyes, I felt balanced and grounded. There was still pressure in my head, but I was no longer short of breath, and the earth around me was still.

Back in our tent later that evening, it felt too soon to go to bed, but I had no energy to read by headlamp. I tried to reflect on the day. As we'd walked back down Lent Hills, Fabian had gestured to the slope that dipped toward where our tents stood like orange bubbles on the dirt. There had been a glacier here, once. I wanted to think about the glaciers. About climate change. If scientists are right, the other glaciers on the mountain will vanish eventually. Soon. From what I'd read, the science is complicated and goes beyond more heat equals less snow when it comes to Kilimanjaro. *Or maybe it doesn't. I wonder if years from now I'll say: Yes, I saw the ice on Kilimanjaro*. My head couldn't handle the direction my mind was going. I surrendered to the serenity of thoughtlessness and then an early sleep.

SHUKA
Advanced Workout Four

Shuka is a Swahili word referring to a sash or decorative piece of cloth worn by many African people. The red and blue plaid variety is popular and is used in several capacities on a Kilimanjaro climb, from mattress covers to tablecloths!

Warm-up		
Foam roller and dynamic	See Appendix A	
Treadmill incline walk	10 mins	With backpack (12 lb), Incline 15, moderate pace
Series One: Repeat the series six times		
1. Jump squats	15	
2. Double stairs	1 min	
3. Calf raises	20/direction	Moderate weight
4. Walkouts	10	
5. Alternating jump lunges	10/side	
Series Two: Repeat the series once		
1. Treadmill incline walk	20 mins	Incline 15, fast pace (no backpack)
Series Three: Repeat the series eight times		
1. Lateral shuffles	30 secs/side	Incline 6, moderate pace

TWO NATURAL STONE PILLARS
MARK THE ENTRANCE.

Heave. Stomp. Heave. Stomp. Heave. Stomp. Heave.

I veered to the right so that the man breathing heavy behind me could maintain his metronomic pace and pass. I was perplexed. *How the hell does he have frost in his beard?* Our team had reconvened with other groups who'd camped elsewhere the night before, and we walked en masse past Shark's Tooth Rock and toward Lava Tower. I looked down to the ground. Rocks, dirt and, indeed, any standing water was frozen into thin sheets of ice, some shattered into pieces from boots or trekking poles.

My trekking poles were folded up and tucked under my arm. The land beneath my feet was at a steady, gradual incline, and I found it more taxing on my body to use the poles than to just let my legs do what I'd spent all year training them to. As we neared the towering rock formation at 4600 metres, I was feeling good – pumped that my headache was gone and that I was actually keeping up with the rest of the team. My winter skin had started to regenerate, and I unwrapped my scarf – cool air on my bare neck – to vent the heat my body was producing.

Our porters were top notch and got to Lava Tower well ahead of other groups to snag a lunch spot directly beneath the rock formation that towered 300 feet above us. A few more ambitious and agile hikers sat on top of it, pointing up and out at things only they could see from their vantage point. Paul and I took a photo in front of the tower and then ducked into the mess tent to eat. The menu was starting to become familiar. Always a hot soup of some kind, followed by lots of meat and lots of starch. Fried chicken, bread, spaghetti and meatballs, potato salad, French fries. These were all fast becoming staples. For lunch that day? I can't remember, but macaroni and cheese is probably a good guess, and even if that's not what it was, it was definitely delicious. And yet, my husband wasn't eating as much as he normally would. I offered him what was left on my plate after I got my fill.

"Nah. I'm good, thanks."

That was a first.

"Are you okay?" I asked.

"Yeah…I'm fine."

I didn't believe him.

"Is that ibuprofen around?" He squinted a little.

Altitude. I grabbed my bag from the corner of the tent and handed him a couple of pills. He took them and chugged back half the water in his bottle.

"Are you all finished, Erinny?" Kijani asked, surprised at the food left on my plate. "Did you like it?"

"Yeah, it was great! Just couldn't fit it all in today. I'm sorry."

"It's okay, Erinny!" He cleared the dishes away. It was time to keep going.

Here was the start of the Western Breach, the path Angela had taken up. It's shorter, steeper and more dangerous, the embankment prone to rock slides

and tumbling boulders as the glaciers dissipate from above it. *Seems about right*, I thought. Angela – an adrenaline junkie whether she wants to admit it or not – would definitely choose that way up. But it was not our path. We'd reached our max elevation for the day and would start another descent, down through the Barranco Valley.

Two natural stone pillars mark the entrance of what is the most majestic place on the mountain, if not on Earth. Fifteen minutes into our walk, the fog came in strong, limiting our view to a few dozen metres. The air became moist enough for us to pull out our rain gear and pack covers. Science fact: mist plus dust makes mud. With the stony path downhill becoming slick, the risk became a trip cut short by a slip and a rolled ankle, or worse. I thanked Angela under my breath for all the calf-raises. The simple move always felt somewhat silly – a spacer, integrated to offer a rest between sets of other more important exercises. It proved that day to be maybe the most important of the bunch. Instead of having to worry about my steps, I could trust my feet enough to allow the privilege of immersing myself in the alien landscape around me.

Colours were delicately muted by the mist, and you could hear water trickling but couldn't see it. The path curved down and around the powerful *Dendrosenecio kilimanjari*, giant groundsels. Trees, technically, whose layers peel back and fold on themselves creating bulky branches. To me, each tree looked more like a cactus with giant, elongated pineapples for arms. They seemed natural and unearthly at the same time. "You don't find these anywhere else," said James. As we moved through, pops of little yellow flowers appeared and disappeared like fairies in the fog. For sure, if there is a place on the planet where fairies exist, it's here.

Fast-forward a couple of hours, and I'd stopped giving a fuck about fairies and the science fiction landscape around me. As the giant groundsels became fewer and fewer, those damned slimy rocks were all that was left. My body shivered from the exertion, as if I'd been holding a plank for hours. In some ways, I had. Stiffly maintaining posture and balance, even my arms hurt from the tense grip I kept on my poles, ready to catch myself in a fall. By the time we could spot the orange specks of our tents set up at the bottom of the valley below, I was exhausted.

Paul and I settled into our tent, careful to leave our wet rain gear under the vestibule and not track any water inside. It was looking to be a chilly night, and we were already pretty damp. Being wet would make it worse.

With time before dinner, we hung out in the mess tent. Rain pattered on the fabric above us and steam rose up from our mugs of hot tea. I brought out the embroidered flower I'd been working on, but my fingers were still too shaky to manage the tiny beads and needle. Krista pulled out a pack of cards and we settled on an easy game of Go Fish. Roman joined the group but wasn't interested in being dealt in. Instead he surprised us all with a magic trick, using my beadwork to guess my card – something no one saw coming from the guy who'd mostly enjoyed chatting about his work up to this point.

When we stepped back out from the tent, it was dusk, the mist gone. Kibo had snuck up behind us, the Goliath mound now looming over our camp. The peak was still a long ways away, but now up instead of out. Directly beneath it, our next day's task stood in plain view: the infamous Barranco Wall.

MBEGE
Advanced Workout Five

Mbege, known as banana beer, is a traditional brew of the Chagga people of Tanzania. The process required to make the drink is one of several steps over several days. Many coffee and waterfall tours on the lower slopes of Kilimanjaro will stop at a local bar offering the opportunity to try it.

Warm-up		
Foam roller	See Appendix A	
Treadmill incline walk	10 mins	With backpack (12 lb), Incline 15, moderate pace
Series One: Repeat the series four times		
1. Walking lunges	1 min	Weighted pack (12 lb)
2. Goblet squat with press-outs	15	Moderate weight
3. Standing palms-in dumbbell press	15	Moderate weight
4. Plank off ball with press-outs	1 min	
Series Two: Repeat the series four times		
1. High knees	30 secs	
2. Jumping-jack planks	50	
3. Skaters	20/side	
Series Three: Repeat the series three times		
1. 3-point mid row	12/side	Moderate to heavy weight
2. Rear delt flys	12	Light to moderate weight
3. Lawnmower	12/side	Moderate to heavy weight
4. Supermans	15	

HIS BODY GAVE IT AWAY DESPITE HIMSELF.

The morning we faced the Barranco Wall, I stepped into my hiking boots and fandangoed out from the tent to look up at a clear blue sky above us and down at an ocean of fluffy white cloud beneath us. A few days in, now, Paul and I had found an order to our morning routine, but despite it we were always last to arrive at breakfast, and thus our team was among the last to leave camp for a 250-metre scramble up a cliff.

Walking toward the base of said cliff, I could trace the single line of hikers, guides and porters, all making their way to the top like a row of ants. Once we were in that line, it felt more like a traffic jam. We moved up the cliffside diagonally in chunks of a few metres at a time, standing around and waiting awkwardly as people bottlenecked at sections requiring deeper lunges or the use of arms.

I grew so accustomed to the constant stop-go-stop that I even missed the much-obsessed-over "Kissing Rock," only realizing that I'd made my way around it after looking back over my shoulder to see another hiker – penguin footed, arms out and chest pressed to a boulder – holding up the line to get a picture of her lips pressed to the stone. *Shit! How did I miss it?* Beneath the somewhat narrow ledge next to the boulder, I saw a second perfectly fine ledge that I'd used for my other foot so I could keep my body straight to the path instead of turning my back to the cliff. *All that anxiety about tumbling to my doom, all for nothing.* Even if someone did slip off the edge while skirting around the curve, there was a guide positioned a few feet below, ready to catch anyone who lost their balance.

While the ascent up the wall was underwhelming, the view along the way was not. It provided a perfect viewpoint of the terrain we'd covered the day before. Cleared of mist and in full colour, the Barranco Valley revealed itself to us, like a woman finally peeking from behind her fan to give you a wink and smile just as you're walking away. I attempted to pinpoint the exact path we'd taken down while waiting for my turn to tackle the next chunk of wall.

After cresting the top, groups rested and snacked. Everyone nearby stopped to cheer as a guide appeared from below, holding the hand of a woman with long grey hair and bright purple leggings. It felt a bit presumptuous to assume the woman needed extra encouragement simply because she was older, but I added a little holler to the ensemble regardless, and the woman accepted our offering graciously.

The tide of clouds had risen the wall with us, blanketing our former camp below and underlining the cone of Mount Meru off to the right. I thought of Ang, Meru having been the first mountain she summited in Africa a decade ago. *Would we even be in Africa at all if it weren't for her?* I turned around to find my husband disrobing down to his sleeveless layer. Despite the slow pace of the climb, he'd somehow worked up a sweat anyway. *That's my man*, I thought, allowing myself a moment to appreciate the physique Ang had contributed to, while Mike joked about Paul bringing the gun show to Kilimanjaro.

From here we went through a series of valleys and hills, up and down and up again. Roman still led the group with Fabian. Music kept Roman in his zone, and he had always at least one bud popped into his ear. From behind I could recognize the beat of a Drake song from my Kili playlist. He emphatically spat out a partial lyric: "You only live once, that's the motto–" The only reason I could hear him was that I was no longer at the back of the pack. Whether my pace had increased or that of my team had decreased, it didn't matter. I was happy to hang out with my travel mates who were fast becoming friends. Mike and Krista walked together just ahead of me down a zigzagging path between rocks, two solar panels strapped to the back of Mike's pack to power the GoPro on his shoulder. As the terrain levelled out ahead of another spike up a short distance away, I decided to bring up something that'd been on my mind.

"Did you guys talk about what you'd do if one of you couldn't summit?" I asked Krista and Mike.

"Yeah," said Mike confidently. "For sure we'd want the other person to still summit. What about you guys?"

I looked behind me. Paul walked farther behind us with James, too far to be a part of the conversation.

"It's something we've definitely talked about, but we've left it as a game-time decision. I mean, who knows what things will be like up there. But ideally we'd want the other to go on anyway."

One last steep pitch brought us up to Karanga Camp. Despite having travelled five kilometres that day, we were not even a few dozen metres higher than our last camp. While everyone got settled, I walked toward another perch, picking up black, shiny pieces of obsidian along the way. Sitting to breathe, I kept my eyes open. Our time on the mountain was more than half done, and I wanted to absorb as much of the views as I could. A tuxedo raven flew in to join me. (It's actually called the white-necked raven, but I like my name better.) The large black bird, spiffy in his white collar, stood on the ground beneath me, looked up, and cocked his head to the side. Lazy clouds enveloped the green canopy far below him, creeping up toward us. I rolled the stones in my palm, evaluating their shapes and colour – one the shape of Shark's Tooth Rock.

"Is it okay if I keep this one?" I asked the bird, holding the triangle out to him between my pointer and thumb. "If it's not okay, make a sound."

He said nothing, and so I slipped the souvenir into my jacket pocket. I waited until the clouds seemed right beneath my feet before heading back to camp.

When I returned to our tents, everyone was inside. From Roman's tent, the faint beat of whatever he was listening to. Given that he wasn't rapping along, I guessed he was asleep. Krista was crying in her tent, Mike trying to console her. I didn't strain to hear what she said to Mike (privacy was hard enough to come by, I wasn't going to eavesdrop), but I hoped my question earlier hadn't triggered something. I sent good vibes in their direction. I couldn't know then, but the tears were not far off for me either.

My bucket of warm water sat untouched on the corner of my tent. I ducked my head in to find Paul with his eyes closed and headphones in. I didn't feel like sleeping, and so I fished the shampoo leaves out of my pack and resolved to wash my hair.

Paul opened his eyes and looked at me.

"Are you doing okay?" I asked.

"Yeah!" he said. "Just listening to some meditations."

An exclamation. A sign that he's trying equally as hard to convince *himself* of something as he is me. He put his ear bud back in and shuffled a bit deeper into his sleeping bag. I watched him. His eyes closed in a squint. His breaths shallow and rapid. A vein in his neck pulsing fast. His body gave it away despite himself. My husband was struggling.

The next day we continued the same up and then down and then up pattern. I felt fine, but I'd gone back to trailing the rest of our team, including Paul, by several dozens of metres.

"I'm sorry," I said to James, apologizing less for my pace and more because he seemed so bored. There was little new flora left to ask questions about.

"*Polepole.* You're okay," he insisted.

A porter who'd finished taking down our sleeping quarters called out from behind us. "*Jambo!*" We shuffled over to make way. This had happened hundreds of times by now and I was left in awe. Every. Time. These men were humble superheroes, our bags on their shoulders instead of capes. They are the only reason this mountain is accessible to lay hikers like myself.

"Do you like your job?" I asked James.

"Very much. I worked a long time to get here."

He explained the years he'd spent first as a porter, working his way up and eventually taking the

training courses to become a guide. He'd summited some 180 times.

James and I caught up to the team at the base of the last steep pitch ahead of Barafu Hut, our last camp before the summit. Paul was pulling out a power bar, Mike grabbing something out of the back of Krista's pack. But I was in *my zone!*

"I'm just going to keep going. Is that okay?" I asked James as he pulled off to the side to join the group. This would technically break the rule of one guide in front, another behind, but the only way left to go was up, and he'd be able to keep his eyes on me. With his go-ahead, I nodded and smiled at Paul while keeping my pace and then started lunging up the boulders of the pitch. Pride fuelled my ascent as I caught up with some of the porters and kitchen staff. They chuckled to one another about me, the *mzungu,* the foreigner. Kijani called out: "Eh! Erinny!" and took it upon himself to pair with me. *Check me out! Climbing with the porters.*

My inflated ego burst with the sound of a voice from behind us: "Coming up on your left!" As I shuffled and looked over, a pair of bare feet in flipflops jumped around me.

"Seriously?! In flip flops?!" I blurted out, incredulous.

The man laughed. "I do this a lot," he said, as he hopped up and away.

Kijani and I continued our pace toward the top of the ridge. I became tired soon after, but there was nowhere to pull over to avoid stalling people behind us. I had to keep going, so I imagined myself back home doing step-ups on the bench near the pond, Angela calling out time on our intervals. In those moments, I'd imagined myself right here, on the mountain, feeling the unrelenting burn in my quads and matching it with unrelenting determination. Pushing through. *I got this.*

At the top, Kijani offered to stop with me for a break. Peering over the edge, I could see the rest of the team starting to make their way up. Switching from a lunge to a walk was all the rest I needed. "Nah, I'm good. Let's keep going." We continued along to where camps were being set up. "You should come this way." Kijani pointed in the direction of our tents a few hundred metres over in a clearing. Off in the distance behind them, Mawenzi towered – Kilimanjaro's second highest cone, dark spikes empty of snow. We'd made our way around the entire southern circuit of the mountain and were now at 4700 metres. Our attempt at the summit was only hours away.

I respectfully declined Kijani's instruction, preferring to wait until the rest of the team assembled. I climbed a large boulder and looked back down the trail, standing on my toes and straining my neck to search for Paul's long, dark hair on the hikers that trudged their way toward me. I don't know how long I waited, but finally I spotted the rest of my team. And then: guilt. Paul was far behind the pack and moved slowly as James kept pace beside him. He was obviously having a hard time. And I had left him to follow my own ego up the hill. *I left him.*

In our tent, Paul admitted to a headache. I gave him painkillers and coached him in how I'd been breathing for the last several days.

"In, two, three, four, five, six, seven, eight."

I held my wrists – smothered in lavender and peppermint oil – above his nostrils.

Is he going to be able to do this? Can I really just leave him here if he can't?

"Out, two, three, four, five, six, seven, eight."

CHAPATI
Advanced Workout Six

*Chapati is a round, flat, unleavened bread that is usually
made of whole-wheat flour and cooked on a griddle with oil.
This is commonly made on Kilimanjaro treks as it requires
few ingredients and is a nice energy source for hikers.*

Warm-up		
Foam roller	See Appendix A	
Treadmill incline walk	10 mins	With backpack (12 lb), Incline 15, moderate pace
Series One: Repeat the series four times		
1. Transition lunges	45 secs/side	Moderate weight
2. Lateral lunges (dynamic)	15/side	Moderate weight
3. Step-ups	15/side	Backpack (12 lb)
Series Two: Repeat the series four times		
1. Alternating bench press	1 min	Moderate weight
2. Push-ups with alternating rotations	8/side	
Series Three: Repeat the series three times		
1. Kneeling single arm shoulder press	12/side	Moderate weight
2. Lateral single foot hops	25/side	
3. Single leg Romanian deadlifts	12/side	Moderate weight

BEFORE WE WERE READY, IT WAS TIME TO MOVE AGAIN.

Paul hardly slept for that handful of hours between dinner and our 11-o'clock wake-up call, so neither did I – unable to do anything but listen to his breathing for signs of trouble, wincing every time he couldn't contain a moan. When it was time to get up, we dug deep into our packs. Oilers jerseys, winter coats, mitts. My usually calm and collected husband tugged furiously at a zipper that wouldn't zip, lifting and slamming the pack against the fabric wall of our tent. I waited patiently for him to stop and then grabbed a bag of rationed candy from my pack, stuffing it into one of my pockets.

True to form, Paul and I were last to enter the mess tent. Not the usual smorgasbord. Hot water, tea bags. A couple of sleeves of digestive biscuits for us to share. Any more food than that would be a burden to our stomachs on the climb. James came into the tent to brief us on what was to come. He told us to put our water bottles in a wool sock to prevent the water from freezing. To take frequent sips from our water bladders to keep hydrated and to prevent the hose from clogging with ice. Then he took our pulse oximeter readings. Unhappy with Paul's first reading, James took his a second time. Satisfied, he wrote the number in the log. It was time to go.

James lined us up outside. We weren't to break from this formation.

"Erinny, you first, behind me."

I smirked. Me up front! Obviously because I had mastered the art of *polepole* and would keep everyone at the most reasonable pace. (Definitely this, and not because I risked splitting the team or wandering off the trail alone in the dark if I were anywhere else in line.) Behind me: Paul, Fabian, Krista, Mike, Roman. At the back: Msaada – formerly known as "man with the goatee" – the porter promoted to guide for the night to cover for Denis, whom we'd lost when Deborah left us what seemed like both forever ago and just yesterday.

I popped in my earbuds, which had been tucked away all week and called up my Kili playlist. Before our short rest earlier that night, I'd added any and every song on my phone that I had ever enjoyed, sometimes twice. The list was now over nine hours long. I hit shuffle (and then skipped the first two songs to come up). Off we went.

James didn't wear a headlamp, instead using the front edge of light from mine to set his pace. Around us, everything we could see appeared in shades of blue and grey. I kept my sight on James ahead of me, the small oxygen tank strapped onto his back, strips of duct tape on his pants like reflectors, his body popping out and back into the shadows. It made me anxious, the same way I feel in open water. But there weren't any sharks up here, and adrenaline buoyed by the sugar from my gummies kept my spirits up. It wasn't a pleasant walk. I had to consciously remind myself that my breathlessness wasn't a failing of my fitness but rather an inevitability in the thinner air. My legs remained strong beneath me. *I wonder what will turn out to be harder*, I pondered. *This or child birth?* (While complicated, the short answer will turn out to be this.)

On the first break I passed around my sweets and gave everyone fist bumps. Paul didn't take a candy. Fabian offered to carry his bag, but he refused. The exhaustion started to creep in by the third break, and I understood that while the idea of a night climb to catch a summit sunrise was a nice idea, what made more sense was that it's better not being able to see the monstrosity of the mountain still left to climb in front of you. The pace James pushed for by stepping ahead of my light became hard to maintain, and I found myself becoming both wearier and warier while trailing him. Suddenly he hopped out of my sight line and I noticed the vomit on the path, sidestepping the pile just on time. "Puke!" I warned those behind me. A short while later we moved over and paused to make way for a guide holding the arm of a woman who heaved and cried as they headed back down. She wouldn't make the summit.

Energy and spirits waned as we criss-crossed up the steep grade of the mountainside. At another break a while later, I could tell that fist bumps weren't welcome anymore. Frankly, my mood wasn't into futile attempts at cheerleading, either. "My hands have never felt this freezing before!" Krista said, and I acknowledged my advantage as someone who spends half of every year in temperatures just like this. I was cold, but that wasn't what was keeping my mind occupied. I turned toward Paul, who shut his eyes tight against the beam of my headlamp. He breathed in through his nose and pushed the air back out through his mouth in quick shushes. When he refused Fabian's second offer to take his pack, I stepped in.

"Give him your bag."

Breaks were kept short to keep us from going stiff. Before we were ready, it was time to move again. I looked back. A snake of tiny lights illuminated the switchbacks. I looked up. Darkness. I realized that I was setting the pace for the several dozen people marching up from behind me. *Or maybe I'm holding dozens of people up*, I reasoned, as a crew from behind us took the opportunity to pass.

While I was able to appreciate the beauty of the moment objectively, in my deepest gut was dread. Since I couldn't keep looking back to Paul without stuttering James's stride, I pulled my earbuds out so I could listen for him. Paul breathed hard through gritted teeth. While taking one lunge slowly after another, I grabbed my water hose and pulled it as far as it would go. Putting the tip in my mouth, I crunched up ice and took a sip. Then I threw it over my shoulder to my husband.

"Drink!"

He grasped for it the way a drowning man flails for the rope, then sucked back water like a man who's just found a bottle in the desert. At every break I asked him if he needed to turn around. Every time, he said no, avoiding eye contact. It became clear. As with him giving up his pack, the responsibility had fallen on me to make the call. If I stopped him, the failure to make it to the top would be on me. If I didn't stop him, I wagered his life.

I started to become angry. *What is it with humans? And our fucking egos that make us feel the need to be on top of everything? Is that the reason I'm doing this? My ego? Putting myself through this. Putting my husband through this. For my ego? I've had a great time, and all the good stuff to see is down there!*

Why am I wasting my energy? Why am I risking my husband's life? What kind of wife does that? Just to say I've been on the top of the highest thing? So what?

The lunges felt really steep. I found myself having to pull myself up with my arms, at times. I could swear that we weren't taking switchbacks but instead were climbing straight up, shortcuts over large boulders to make up for time. I cursed James in my head for not offering more encouragement from up front. *He hasn't been saying anything!* In hindsight, encouragement from him at this point was a stupid expectation, lest I forget he was climbing the same mountain.

Bigger than anger, fear. While I waited to catch the *thud* of Paul's body collapsing to the ground behind me, I debated if and when to turn around. If I could decide on a very specific sign, I would know exactly where the line was.

And then I looked up to the sky. The moon had popped up to the left of Mawenzi. A perfect Cheshire-cat grin. Tangerine, the colour of the flowers we'd brought to Angela before leaving. If nothing else, I didn't want to disappoint her. The moon was my sign, I decided, that it was safe to keep going. Suddenly I could hear her voice in my head, cheering us on in the same way she had as we pushed though the last seconds of a set of jump lunges or planks or mountain climbers. "Yes, Erinne! Amazing! You got this!"

The lunges became shorter, and then fewer, the heavily trodden dirt transformed to small gravel the higher we went. Each step became worth only half as much as our boots slid backward.

Stomp, slide.

Stomp, slide.

Faintly, and then louder, I heard hoots and hollers from above. Climbers ahead of us were starting to crest the ridge. Quickly after, the darkness ahead of me was broken by a horizontal layer of light followed by the shadow of the wooden slats that marked Stella's Point.

"I can see the top!" I shouted.

From behind Paul I could hear Mike as he fed off those words and used them to propel Paul forward.

"We're almost there, Paul. You got this, man!"

We crested Stella's Point shortly after, and everyone was game for fist bumps again. Paul had disappeared somewhere, though. I found him next to Fabian, leaning up against a rock on a natural stone bench. Tears leaking from underneath his sunglasses.

"Congratulations," I said softly. He stood up and leaned in to kiss me between sobs. I kissed him back while at the same time tilting my chin to avoid brushing up on the sheet of snot slowly freezing to his collar. By now the sun had started to rise behind us.

"You okay?" I asked.

"Yeah!" Paul coughed. It was starting to sound watery. But we were at the top and just around the corner. Or so I thought. Had I known in that moment that Uhuru Peak – the highest point on the mountain and ultimate destination – was still a good forty-five minutes away, I might have made a different call. But I didn't know.

"Alright. Let's finish this."

It took only minutes for me to start second guessing my decision for us to continue from Stella's Point to Uhuru Peak. Now that Paul was no longer walking behind me in the dark, I could see his condition. He was a zombie. His face pale. Almost swollen. He continued to cough. I worried about the physiological effects I couldn't hear or see going on under his skull.

At this point, teams and lines had spread out. The rest of our group had moved ahead with Fabian while James stayed in the middle and Msaada behind with us. I followed Paul's path in the dirt. Instead of footprints, he left two strips where his feet dragged, outlined by two thinner strips, the marks of his trekking poles that he pulled behind him. The lines zigzagged across the top as Paul continuously redirected his course.

While evaluating and re-evaluating my husband's state, I did my best to also recognize that I was on top of Mount Kilimanjaro. I had done the work to get here, and here I was. *Check me out. On top of Kilimanjaro.* We were blessed with perfect weather. The snow that had covered the peak a week prior was almost gone, and the glaciers stood solid on the slopes beneath us. Sheets of ancient ice blended seamlessly into the sea of clouds behind them. Far off in the distance, Meru again.

Still, I grew more anxious at each turn and hill that didn't reveal the next set of wooden slats marking Uhuru Peak. Paul, with every step, looked as though he were catching himself on one leg after the knee giving out on the other. We were pushing it. My water hose frozen solid at this point, I got out my socked water and gratefully handed off my bag to Msaada when he offered. Pulling up beside Paul, I handed him the bottle.

"Drink."

He did.

"We can turn around at any time. We've made it to the top. We don't have to go all the way to the sign."

"No."

I looked ahead a dozen metres or so to James, who kicked through the sand like a kid through a puddle as he sauntered forward to the peak for his hundred and umpteenth time. He turned around to check on us, and I faintly pointed to Paul as if to say, "Maybe you should look more closely." James didn't take my hint and I grew angry again that he was not taking more charge, not seeing in Paul what I thought was obvious. Later, I would be angry with myself for not making it clear to James that I thought this was what he should have done.

Just one more hill.

One more.

I kept telling myself that if the marker didn't show up this time, we were stopping. Every minute at this elevation would take its toll if altitude sickness was indeed what Paul was dealing with.

One more.

One –

And finally: the marker. Uhuru Peak.

Well, two markers, actually, to facilitate faster pictures. Between those two markers, though, a safe space, like we'd entered the eye of a storm.

There was a stillness to the air.

A quiet.

Paul and I were afforded a pause against the urgency of his condition. "Thank you," I whispered aloud to Kilimanjaro. She'd granted my request.

As we neared, we passed Roman, who'd already had his solo photo-op with the sign, proudly holding out the beverage he'd carried all the way up, as if it was the drink that got him to the top and not his own preparation, determination and rap-music strategy.

I found Krista and Mike both taking in the

moment as best they could, facing out toward the southern icefield. I pulled out my phone and took a video, filming their responses to the question: "How do you feel?" Krista had a headache. "Happy I made it. Ready to go back down." She gave me a thumbs up with a smile and grimace at the same time. Mike coughed in a cloud of dust kicked up from other trekkers celebrating. It was the hardest thing physically – and mentally – that he'd ever accomplished. "At any moment you can just say: Fuck it, I'm done." By the time the video capture bounced around and back to my husband, he was snacking on a protein bar, eyes glossy and voice raspy, standing precariously close to the edge of the ridge. Fabian had strategically positioned himself between Paul and the long drop toward Kibo's volcanic ash pit.

"We made it," I said.

Paul cleared his throat. "I definitely didn't make it look easy," he replied.

My arm extended as far as I could reach, I ended the video trying to capture a kiss but instead got the sound of a smooch with a shot of the sun in blue sky.

Our team gathered for a group shot at the sign, and then Paul and I got our turn alone. We pulled off our winter coats to reveal our Oilers jerseys.

"Hey look – more Canadians!" Another group at the top chirped at us. "Got the wrong team, though."

"We make it to the top, the Oilers make it to the playoffs next season. That was our deal with the universe." (The Oilers didn't make the playoffs that season.) Our fellow compatriots, despite their

allegiance to Toronto, then passed us their Canadian flag to use in our photos.

It had taken us seven hours to get here – Uhuru Peak, the highest point on the continent – and we only stayed maybe fifteen minutes. The pause Kibo had granted us over, I looked at Paul. Eyes staring at nothing as he swayed in place. When I asked him about that moment later, he explained how he'd never felt an emptiness like the one on top of Kilimanjaro. That there was a peace in having been drained of all energy, of having no thoughts. This would make me scared because it sounded like how one might feel when they've given themselves over to death. And indeed, in those final moments at the top, I couldn't sense his spirit anywhere near him. We had to get down. *Now.*

UGALI
Advanced Workout Seven

Ugali is a common food eaten in central and eastern Africa. It is a dish often made from maize flour or millet flour, cooked in boiling water or milk to create a stiff dough-like consistency, and served with salad.

Warm-up		
Foam roller	See Appendix A	
Treadmill incline walk	10 mins	With backpack (12 lb), Incline 15, moderate pace
Series One: Repeat the series four times		
1. Walking lunges	1 min	Weighted pack (15 lb)
2. Back lunge with hop	15/side	Moderate weight
3. Lateral step-ups	20/side	
Series Two: Repeat the series four times		
1. Single leg goblet squats	15/side	Moderate weight
2. Single leg glute bridge pulses	20/side	
3. Long jumps	20	
Series Three: Repeat the series three times		
1. Mountain climbers	30 secs	
2. Side plank with leg lifts	30 secs/side	
3. Plank with alternating shoulder taps	15/side	
4. Skipping/jump rope	1 min	

MY TOES TOOK IT ESPECIALLY HARD.

Looks like a bear, I thought. Two round, stone ears and a snout. The face peeked out at me from a set of boulders farther below from where I'd fallen. Back on the slope beneath Stella's Point, the scree provided a new challenge as every step turned into a skid. Step, skid, step, skid, skid, skid, swish, swish, swish. My hips had taken over, my body reverting to a more familiar downhill habit – skiing. It was just as I caught myself having fun that I biffed it, landing hard on my tailbone, sand shooting up underneath my winter coat. Bits of sand and tiny rock chips found their way up and down between the cracks of my tucked layers and poked at my lower back.

I looked up the hill, searching for Paul. The husk of my husband also sat in the scree, hands tight around the top of his walking poles that were pressed out in front of him. Insurance against tumbling into a full log-roll down the hill. Msaada also sat, halfway between Paul and me.

The rest of our team was far below us on their way back to camp at Barafu. I grabbed my water, choosing a small swig given how far away camp still seemed to be. "At any point you can just say: Fuck it, I'm done," Mike had said at the top. He wasn't entirely right. If there were a way to quit in that moment, sitting in the dirt under direct sun, I would've done it. I imagined an army chopper hovering above us, a rope dropped out to wrap around my arms and legs. But there is no turning around on the descent. And there was still so much descent left to go.

That man sitting above me isn't my husband. I don't know where he went, but that's not him. What long-term consequences would there be for Paul? Instead of worrying about whether or not I was making the right decision, now that it had been made, I worried about how I would answer to our family when they asked: Why? Was the success of the summit worth what we'd have to pay for it? *What the fuck have I just done?*

A shadow appeared from behind me. Paul had made his way down to where I sat.

"You alright?" he asked. He was obviously exhausted, but his eyes were clear and he looked directly into mine. *There you are.* I realized that maybe I was overreacting. (Give me a break. With all this talk about how badly Paul was affected by the altitude, chances are, so was I.)

"Yeah," I said, pushing myself up off the ground.

Together, we semi-skied down spurts of the mountain at a time. Step-sliding until our legs gave out. Sitting until there was enough energy to stand and step-slide again. The tents of our camp down below slowly but surely grew bigger and bigger. Eventually, a group of porters came up to relieve Msaada of his duties. They formed a semi-circle around us, the man with a skull on his toque holding me up by my left arm. Like angels, they guided us the rest of the way back. What should have taken us two hours had taken us four.

Back at Barafu, our fellow summiters were already asleep in their tents. James handed me a cup of mango juice and a happy congratulations. If there was any pride in my ascent, it was buried deep beneath the rubble of my emotions. Also, I was still (admittedly unrightfully) pissed with James for not checking on Paul. I forced a smile and went straight to the tent. Paul followed. There was only about forty-five minutes left before we were scheduled to get up for the next portion of the descent.

The second Paul zipped the flap of our tent shut, I erupted into tears.

"I was so scared," I cried.

"It's okay. We made it."

Paul had no energy to console me, but he listened as I tried to piece together all my feelings. I fell asleep whimpering. When a porter rapped on our tent seemingly seconds later, "Time to go, Paul and Erinny" my eyelashes were crusted with dirt and salt. The rest was not enough, but it was all we got. My cry had released enough pressure for me to continue, though I felt more numb than anything as we rolled and stuffed our winter gear back to the bottom of our bags and made our way back out into the sunshine. The cook team offered us a huge lunch, but I mostly didn't eat. Despite being hungry, it had been a week of starchy, carby, greasy foods, and they'd become unappetizing. I felt guilty about it, but the thought of fried chicken made me gag.

The path off the mountain was a straight line down compared to the meandering, roundabout way we'd gone up. At first the ground was a manageable grade on packed dirt as we passed back through the alpine zone. Slowly, rocks sprouted flowers and shrubs stretched into trees. Just as I started to feel despondent, we got to camp. Or *a* camp, rather. My heart broke when I realized the men setting up tents weren't our porters. This was just a break, and our camp was at least two more hours away. From

there, the path down became rocky and steep. A reverse scramble, at times. I eventually learned to step down gently, to find the best footing and minimize the impact on my knees. But by then it was too late. I'd spent too many kilometres ripping heavy boots up off the ground only for my feet to snap like magnets back to the earth with every small step downward. My toes took it especially hard.

While the team had mostly stuck together for a large portion of this second round of descent, ultimately we split back into our usual groupings, the solidarity at the summit not enough to convince our new friends to extend the day any longer than they had to. This time, though, Paul and I left no more than a handful of metres between us. *Polepole*, we helped each other down the sketchier passes of a trail that never seemed to end.

Eventually I started to see mirages of our camp and grew irritated by the cycles of relief followed by grief. The orange tents peeked through the bush only to vanish as we turned the corner. *This is hell*, I thought. *Somewhere up there we died. And now we are in hell. An eternal decent.* But then...my angel. Man in the skull toque appeared from around a bend. He took my bag and my arm, and walked me the rest of the way to camp.

It had been another four hours or so since we'd left Barafu, making our total hiking time that day fifteen hours. After signing in Mweka Camp's logbook, I looked up. At just over 3000 metres, we were back in the upper ranges of rainforest. Bearded lichen hung from tree branches, fluffy like green ostrich feathers. Kibo was no longer visible. Sighing, I made my way to the mess tent for a final dinner with the team. I'd resigned myself to another grilled cheese or potato salad. But what a surprise! Our cook Brian treated us to a traditional Tanzanian meal.

"What is this called?" One of us asked Kijani about the aromatic stewed meat and vegetable dish in front of us.

"African food," he replied. We looked at each other.

"Okay."

We gorged. Later, bellies plump, we heard men singing outside. Voices grew louder until Brian, Kijani, man with the skull on his toque and a few other porters burst into our tent.

"Cakeeeey, Cakeey-o! Cakeeeey, Cakeey-o!"

Brian presented us with a cake, iced in white, Uhuru peak piped on in yellow and "Congratulations" in red. Truth? It tasted terrible. I could only manage a few polite bites, blaming it on too much ugali. And yet, of all the cakes in my life, it will be one of the few I'll remember into my old age.

ACACIA
Advanced Workout Eight

The acacia, an iconic umbrella-shaped tree, is a symbol of renewal, fortitude and pureness. Over time, African acacia trees have adapted to harsh climates by maximizing sun-capturing surface area, while maintaining small leaves. Depictions of these trees are common in many of the Kilimanjaro paintings and other art pieces you're likely to come across during your travels.

Warm-up		
Foam roller and dynamic	See Appendix A	
Treadmill incline walk	10 mins	With backpack (20 lb), Incline 15, moderate pace
Series One: Repeat the series four times		
1. Double stairs	1 min	
2. Burpees	10	
3. Single stairs	1 min	
4. Wide-narrow jump squats	15 each	
5. Double stairs	1 min	
6. Long jumps	20	
7. Single stairs	1 min	
8. Side-to-side jump lunges	15/side	
Series Two: Repeat the series once		
1. Treadmill incline walk	20 mins	Incline 15, fast pace
Series Three: Repeat the series eight times		
1. Lateral shuffles	30 secs/side	Incline 6, moderate pace

I WONDERED WHY I HAD YET TO FEEL LIKE I'D ACCOMPLISHED ANYTHING GR – GAH!

I woke up the next morning having slept hard. Wincing, I wiggled my toes slowly and decided it was probably best to not remove my socks at all until we were back at the hotel later. The trek was nearly done, but there was still much more to go today.

After packing up our gear for the final time and bidding our tent adieu with a salute, we entered the mess tent for breakfast and started the task of divvying up cash for the porters' and guides' tips. A task that was already going to be hard, due to complete mental exhaustion, was made harder by our earlier screw up of having not come with enough American cash. Everyone else – Roman even carrying tips for a full climb on behalf of Deborah – had their money ready. We threw our Tanzanian shillings into the mix and still didn't have our fair share. After too much math to divide two currencies into the right amounts in the right envelopes, and a promise to repay Krista and Mike for covering what we did not have, the tips were sorted and we could finally leave.

Emerging from the tent, the rest of camp had been completely taken down, save for the toilet tent, which Paul attempted to duck into before I called him back. "What are you doing?" The porters stood around anxiously waiting for the tipping ceremony. "They need to get going!" Paul grimaced and we joined the rest of the group as Roman led a tip-of-the-cap thank you and gave the envelopes to the designated receivers, shaking their hands. Kijani then made his way into the middle of the circle and led our support crew in the classic Kilimanjaro song that I'd heard in several YouTube videos. I didn't understand the words but picked up on the names of all the camps that we'd visited up to Uhuru Peak and back. The song segued into another Tanzanian classic first sung in the 80s by Kenyan band "Them Mushrooms."

Jambo! Jambo bwana! Hello! Hello sir!
Habari gani? Mzuri sana! How are you?
　Very well!
Wageni, mwakaribishwa!
　Guests, you are welcome!
Kilimanjaro? Hakuna matata!
　Kilimanjaro? No trouble!

Kijani pulled us into the dance and we hobbled as best we could along with our porters until they stopped singing. Then like a reverse flash mob, they picked up the gear and darted down the trail while a few stayed back to handle packing up the mess tent.

The day's walk was bittersweet, punctuated with moments of pure agony each time I stubbed my toe on the tree roots that segmented the path like rungs on a ladder. Still decompressing from the day before, I wondered why I had yet to feel like I'd accomplished anything gr – *Gah!* My boot got caught on another root, bringing my attention back to the rainforest. Among the monkeys and flowers, these were my final moments on the mountain, and I told myself to absorb whatever I could in any of the pores I had left that weren't caked with dir – *Arg!* Another root, and I could feel my left big toenail floating in my sock.

Paul, meanwhile, walked a short distance ahead of me. We were away from the immediate danger of altitude now, but he was still obviously uncomfortable. Coughing, sweating, spitting. Reluctantly admitting to a headache. He pulled off the trail into the bush for a pee, and I waited, back toward him, the rest of team continuing ahead. I turned when I heard him chuckle and curse.

We've all been there. You think it's just gas and then, whoops! Unfortunately for Paul, he was in the Kilimanjaro rainforest, boots on and pants around his knees, his spare clothes long gone down the trail. We stood motionless, unbelieving for a while, as other pockets of hikers passed us periodically, all respectfully looking off in the opposite direction. *Was it the Tanzanian food from last night? Did he miss a spot with the hand sanitizer before eating? Or is this something more serious? A red-flag symptom of some sort?* I have never needed Google more.

Whatever it was, we needed to tackle the more immediate problem at hand. Remember I said we'd use the Swiss Army Knife one more time? Well, this was that time. Paul cut and ripped away his soiled boxers. He'd make the rest of the descent commando, but what to do with the dirty drawers? I couldn't bear to just chuck them into the forest. That would be a disrespect to the mountain, to the country and the locals who'd made our trip possible. We found a small bag in Paul's daypack. He tied the remnants of his undergarment tightly in the plastic and got back on the path. Soon after, James caught up with us and offered to carry the extra bag, not knowing where it came from. Paul refused. When

the last of the porters passed us, James tore the bag from Paul's grasp and handed it to one – the extra man we'd picked up at Londorossi Gate. Paul will feel forever connected to the man who helped him out when the mountain had literally stripped him to his most vulnerable. We caught up to the rest of the team, who at least pretended to not know what had happened.

I could swear our pace going down the trail was slower than it was going up. We were passed several times by locals who lived on the mountain's lower regions, young men and women carrying materials down from the slopes, who looked at us no differently than they would passing a truck on the street. Another walk that was supposed to take only a few hours was stretching into, well, we wouldn't know how long until we finally got to the end. Paul, despite his condition, fought through it without complaining. He was zoned-in to the descent. I was not as stoi – *fuck! WHY?!* – roaring in pain as my left toe took a beating with every step.

Finally, the path became a road, and that road led to the exit gate. Waiting for us at the bottom was Deborah, who had had a wonderful time exploring other sites of the region with a small group of ladies who'd left the same day she had. Us sorry sights likely validated her decision to stop when she did.

After sealing our successful summit attempt with a final signature in the park's log, we piled into a small bus. Driving past the small communities back to Moshi, I watched as locals went about their daily lives, a part of which includes the weary stares of tourists fresh off a once-in-a-lifetime journey. The dichotomy of these two energies seemed surreal, but in reality, commonplace experiences cross paths with extraordinary experiences all the time. The person climbing the stairs because it's a quick way to get to work passes by the person who is on their tenth round of them in preparation for a life-changing hike. Suddenly our stench materialized in the confines of the vehicle, and we scrambled to open all the windows.

We arrived back at the hotel a while later and gathered around the table in the same common area where we'd met for the first time just over a week ago. A waiter came by, but no one was in the mood for a beer. James asked us to spell our names as he wrote out and handed us each our certificates, congratulating us yet again on our success. With the paperwork wrapped up, it was time to say goodbye to our teammates, who were staying at different hotels. I didn't cry but was definitely choked up. I'm sure Mike would be okay to admit that he was watery-eyed too as we all said farewell, with offers to join each other in our respective parts of the world any time in the future. Our journey together cemented a bond that would connect us regardless of how much or little we'd keep in touch.

Upstairs, back in our room, Paul and I undressed quickly and headed to the shower. Paul got straight into the stream while I stood off to the side, waiting for the water to heat up.

I waited.

And waited.

Looking up to the hot water tank in the high corner of the ceiling, I realized the staff hadn't turned on the heater until we'd arrived. There was only cold water. Paul didn't care, but I couldn't do it. I had gone this long without a shower, I could wait another hour.

The next day I found myself being prematurely nostalgic for the cacophony of Moshi, full-blast on the other side of our room's bathroom wall. On my knees next to the tub, I slid my scarf into a shallow inch of warm water. It oozed brown. Fingertips spread lightly across the top of the floating fabric, I jiggled my hands and the water got darker.

I drained the tub and then filled it again, this time adding soap from the dispenser above the sink. I rubbed sections of the scarf together and then jiggled it some more.

Drained the tub again.

Filled it again. Another inch or so of fresh water to rinse.

One more time.

Satisfied, I wrung my scarf out, foot by foot, then left the bathroom to hang it on a chair to dry.

Paul lay in bed, eyes closed and head in his hands. I'd reprised my role of "call maker," this time trying to decide the line between waiting it out and taking him to a hospital for a proper medical evaluation. According to everything I'd googled, the altitude sickness should get better once you get to lower ground. We'd been back for a full day, and still he groaned in pain any time he switched positions. But he insisted every time I brought it up that he was okay.

I looked at my scarf and admired my laundering skills. Then I picked up my whole pack and brought it to the bathroom, unloading all the dirty clothes onto the floor. I filled the tub with another few inches of clean water and threw my socks and underwear in for their turn.

I still felt conflicted about our climb. I'd expected jubilation at the end, but instead I felt...what did I feel? *Shame? Why shame?* Because we hadn't made it back down in good enough shape to be able to take our coffee tour today? Because my husband lay in so much pain, still, and it was my fault for not stopping him from ascending all the way?

I pulled the socks out and drained the tub. Filled it again. One piece at a time, I washed my pants and shirts.

Okay, maybe it wasn't fair to shoulder the responsibility for Paul's decision, and missing a coffee tour wasn't that big a deal. But it wasn't like we'd done anything all that unique to be proud of. There were dozens of climbers at the top when we summited, and dozens more before we got there ourselves that morning. More the day before that, and the day before that. There were likely dozens more people on the summit right now.

Drained the tub.

Filled it again.

I replayed moments from the summit in my head and then got to an exchange I'd had with James.

"A great achievement," he'd said.

"Thank you. Quite the challenge," I'd replied offhandedly.

To which he said, "Exactly."

Exactly.

Exactly.

The challenge was the point.

Sure, we were not unique in our effort nor in our success. But success isn't defined as being the only one at the top. We'd set ourselves a challenge, we'd worked hard to prepare ourselves for it, and then we'd done it. Together. And we're bound to face more challenges together, both ones we'll choose and others that will be chosen for us. For sure, part of climbing Kilimanjaro was to see what exactly our bodies could do, but we also wanted to see how we could manage the challenge as partners. I compared how I thought the climb would go with how it actually went. Our journey had flipped the script on the narrative I'd been expecting to tell. I was the one who was supposed to struggle, to barely make it. Paul was supposed to valiantly help me to the top. But while at the time it felt like Paul's success had been reliant on me, it worked both ways. Whether my worry for his condition was warranted or not, it kept me occupied and distracted from my own body, and that is likely why I got to the top.

Our summit wasn't about other people. Our summit was about us. Well, us and one other person. I walked back through our room. Paul was snoring, which meant he'd found enough relief from the pain to finally sleep. I stepped outside to the railing and caught a tiny glimpse of Kilimanjaro through a space between the clouds while I waited for my phone to connect. I texted Angela.

Made it to the top and back!

IT'S SO MUCH SWEETER THAT
THEY DO IT FOR THEMSELVES.

Having trained clients for nearly half my life, I've had the pleasure of watching men and women of all ages gain physical and mental strength, confidence and endurance. I've witnessed them break personal fitness records, lose weight, build muscle, win races, reach summits and live bucket-list dreams. In short, I've seen exercise enhance – and in some cases entirely change – people's lives.

But even after all these years, I still get nerves of anticipation every time a client is about to live out that moment they have been training so hard for. It's the same irrational conversation I have with myself before I embark on a fitness adventure.

Do they feel prepared? Are they going to make it to the summit? Will the altitude be a problem? Are they going to enjoy the climb? Did I give them enough information on what to eat?

Eventually, I pull myself together and remember the dedication and hard work that went into their training, and that gives me more peace of mind.

Don't be silly, Ang. They executed the plan and are absolutely ready for this! No matter what the outcome, they can be proud of the training that went into this huge fitness goal. All that hard work will pay off. They have earned this!

Ang, trust the process.

I'm normally the one doing the reassuring, but sometimes I need a little reassuring too. As the trainer, you want it so bad for your clients that you almost wish you could just do it for them. But of course, it's so much sweeter that they do it for themselves.

Every day I would wake up and check my phone, sitting bedside with Larry (my cat), for a text-message update. I assume this is how my family and friends feel when I am away hiking in Africa. It's so much easier when you are the one away, not the one at home waiting! And then it's text messages like this, from Erinne and Paul on August 7, 2015, that put things back into perspective:

> Hello Angela, Paul and Erinne here from Karanga camp! All the squats and lunges have sure helped us get here. We are scheduled to walk to the summit tomorrow night and we are feeling pretty good!

With a huge smile, I immediately thought about the months and months of squats and lunges they executed with zero complaint. If you're currently following the plan laid out in this book, you will fully understand what I'm talking about! Right from Day One they understood the importance of repetition in training due to the repetitive nature of hiking. I always knew the workout was extra intense when Paul's smile grew even wider and he chuckled a little bit under his breath. Erinne's tell was when she would stop relying on my counting and start counting herself. She wasn't going to do an extra rep! Her questions tended to lessen as the workout intensity increased, as well. There wasn't energy for chitchat when the legs started to burn.

I was thrilled to hear that they were feeling good and sounded confident in their bodies. They'd earned those strong legs. I replied in my "coolest" texting voice:

> Hi you guys!!! I think of you
> every day and count the time change
> forward to get an idea of where
> you might be at in the moment. So
> happy to hear from you! Have a great
> summit!!!

I could have kept it to one exclamation point, but my excitement got the better of me. I received a second message back.

> Thanks Angela! Whenever we
> feel tired we just imagine your voice
> in our heads. We start the trek to
> summit in 14 hours. Supposed to
> take anywhere from 6–8 hrs to get to
> the top. Even so, the whole trek has
> already been a success. Off we go to
> Barafu!

I put my trainer hat back on and replied one more time, trying to keep it together and remind them to stay in the moment.

> Can't wait to hear from you! Enjoy
> the journey up! The scree on the way
> down feels like you are surfing down
> the mountain. Have fun and take it
> all in! So happy you both are doing
> well with the altitude.

When it came to Erinne and Paul, I had calculated in advance, factoring in the drastic time difference, the exact day and approximate time they would reach Uhuru Peak. When my phone did not notify me with an update on the day I had anticipated it would, I tried to keep positive. I was fully aware that weather, cell reception or adding an extra acclimatization day could be possible reasons for not having heard from them yet. Not to mention the scenario where they would likely be a tad on the tired side and would send a note once they were safely down from the mountain, showered and celebrating with a couple of cold Tusker beers. I held onto the last scenario and waited patiently.

I was in the middle of training another client on August 10 when my phone finally lit up with another message from Paul and Erinne. I couldn't respond, out of respect for my client's time, but I was thrilled to receive the news.

> Made it to the top and back! Legs
> have been doing great – hardly any
> sore muscles thanks to your prepar-
> ation – thank you, thank you, thank
> you! No way we could've done it
> without your training, and happy to
> help maintain your 100% success rate
> for clients climbing Kili!

I let out a little yelp and explained the situation to my client, who was also a mountain trekker. He fully understood how exciting the news was. After the session was complete, I immediately pulled out my phone. Like the feeling when you meet a friend you have not seen in years at the airport, I was so delighted. Tears pooled in my eyes! I responded with the biggest sense of relief and an immense sense of respect for the two of them. It takes a great deal of strength, courage and training dedication to *attempt* a summit like this one, let alone make it. I can provide all the tools in the world, but if they had not used them, it would not have been a success.

> Erinne and Paul!! I've been waiting to hear from you. I even kept my cell phone next to the bed! I'm so proud of you! Congratulations on an incredible accomplishment. You earned this! I can't wait to hear all about it. It has been such a pleasure to work with you two and see the progress week-to-week, month-to-month.

And then the text message you don't want to get (but at least I knew the outcome was okay).

> We didn't even check for reception at the top – Paul was so sick. I was terrified that it was HACO and made sure we descended almost as soon as we got to the top. He's resting now, and I'm about to do the same. Will be in touch as soon as we get back home ☺

I had so many questions and wanted to know every detail of the trek, but it was not the time to get into it. I was just so grateful to hear that they were down safely, despite the altitude sickness.

> Oh my goodness I have so many questions. I'm glad Paul is okay. Get some well-deserved sleep/rest. Can't wait to see you guys!

The days passed and Erinne and Paul finally arrived home safe and sound after summiting Kili and then spending some earned beach time in Zanzibar to recover and celebrate.

Once they got home, I could have listened to their stories all day! Hearing the details of their journey brought back memories and created new images in my mind of what it was like to summit from a different route. Their journey was challenging, and at times a bit worrisome, but that truly comes with the territory when you are hiking at high altitudes. I think Paul and Erinne had a good understanding of that before they left, but having been through it, I think they have an even stronger appreciation for what they actually accomplished. There is a reason only fifty per cent of people make it to the summit.

When I first met Erinne and Paul, I felt confident that Paul would continue to incorporate fitness into his life post-Kilimanjaro, as he was an avid hockey player and had played sports all his life. I did not anticipate that Erinne, having started relatively sedentary, would embrace the exercise and want to continue after the climb. Upon her return from Africa she dove deep into the editing of *Reality Fitness* and at the same time committed to keeping up her fitness level. I was thrilled! Erinne and Paul jumped right back into their regular time slot on Fridays with me. She held true to her game plan and kept her training up all through her first pregnancy. As soon as she was given medical clearance after delivery, Erinne was back to working out, and excited about it. It was obvious that training for Kilimanjaro was a catalyst for a more active lifestyle. It's now three years (almost to the day, as I write this) since they were in Africa, and Erinne and Paul still incorporate fitness into their lives. As their trainer and friend, this impresses me even more than the trek itself. They are a great team, and it's such a pleasure to see them continue with their fitness endeavours together. Every day they set a healthy example for their beautiful little girl. I can't wait to see what they do next!

As a trainer, I am very happy to see clients meet goals and accomplish amazing things like Kilimanjaro, but the true reward is when clients incorporate fitness into their lives because they see the value it has beyond the bucket list, allowing them to feel better and do more. Fitness changes lives! It's wonderful to see clients feeling strong, to see them with more energy, taking time for themselves, to feel healthy, happy and confident in their own skin.

Uhuru means "freedom" in Swahili, which is fitting as I have always said to my clients "fitness is freedom." A fit body offers so many more opportunities to see the world from unique perspectives, like the roof of Africa. With dedication to your training, some mental grit and a little altitude luck on your side, you too will be snapping photos next to Kilimanjaro's signature sign marking Uhuru Peak.

THOSE BOOTS TOOK HER FATHER
TO THE TOP OF KILIMANJARO.

A few years after our summit, on a mid-November morning, I watched my year-old daughter – in her leopard-print onesie – playing among the bags and snowboarding gear waiting to be loaded at our front door. Mom and Dad were going to catch opening day at Marmot Basin in Jasper National Park. Anouk, still early to walking and not ready for skis, would stay with Papi and Pippa for the weekend. She peered into her father's hiking boots and then roared into them. (She'd been testing the sound of her voice in different receptacles.) Hearing whatever it is she was hoping for, she sat and then lifted her little leg, foot hovering midway up the back of the boot. Not able to get high enough to put the boot on, she switched legs, tried the other one. No dice. She looked at me to see if I'd help her get the boot on but quickly lost interest while I debated whether or not it was sanitary for her to even be touching them.

She doesn't know or understand or care, yet, that those boots took her father to the top of Kilimanjaro. When she's old enough to know and understand, she still may or may not care. But my hope is that regardless of how she feels about our trip, we will have raised her to seek out accomplishments of all kinds, including those that push her body to its limits. I hope that we continue to lead her in that direction by example. Lucky for all of us, we'll have Ang close by to help make whatever physical feats we dream up a reality.

THE WORKOUTS

1889
Beginner Workout One

Warm-up		
Stairs or treadmill walk	5-10 mins	Light to moderate pace
Series One: Repeat the series twice		
1. Squats	15	Light weight
2. Stationary lunges	10/side	
3. Stairs	2 mins	
Series Two: Repeat the series twice		
1. Single leg bicep curls	10/side	Light weight
2. Plank off hands with alternating knee-pulls to the chest	10/side	
3. Stairs	2 mins	
Series Three: Repeat the series once		
1. Walking	15 mins	Light to moderate pace

SERIES ONE
(Repeat the series twice)

1. SQUATS

Targeted Muscles: Front and back of legs, buttocks

Stand with your feet shoulder-width apart (the insides of your feet should be in line with the outsides of your shoulders). Bend at your hips and knees to lower into a squat position (as if you're about to sit in a chair) until your thighs are just past parallel to the floor. If you have knee problems, do not go past parallel. Keep your knees over your ankles (you should be able to see your toes throughout the entire movement). Maintain good posture by keeping your chest up as you stand up, pushing through your heels. Complete 15 repetitions.

2. STATIONARY LUNGES (LEFT)

Targeted Muscles: Front and back of legs, buttocks

Take a large step backward and bend both knees to 90°. Your front knee should track over your front ankle, and your back knee should track underneath your hip and be as close to the floor as possible without touching it. Slowly transition from the lowered position to the upright position without moving your feet. Push yourself up each time, applying pressure through your front heel. Keep the motion controlled and slow. Complete 10 repetitions, then switch legs.

3. STAIRS

Targeted Muscles: Front and back of legs, buttocks, calves, your heart

Walk, jog or run up and down a flight of stairs. The objective is to pace yourself so you can maintain movement for the duration of the exercise, without stopping. Complete 2 minutes.

1 2 3

SERIES TWO
(Repeat the series twice)

1. SINGLE LEG BICEP CURLS
Targeted Muscles: Front of arms, abdominals, buttocks, calves, upper back

Holding a weight in each hand, arms at your sides, balance on one foot and slowly raise both wrists up toward your shoulders simultaneously (bicep curl). Lower the weights back down to your hips. Complete ten repetitions, then switch to balance on the other leg and repeat.

2. PLANK OFF HANDS WITH ALTERNATING KNEE-PULLS TO CHEST (LEFT)

Targeted Muscles: Shoulders, abdominals, upper back, hip flexors

From a plank position off your hands (see Base Plank [off Hands], opposite), very slowly bring one knee in under your chest, pause, then extend the leg back. Repeat the same movement pattern on the other side. Keep your hips as still as possible to get the most out of this exercise. Complete 10 repetitions (alternating) on each side.

BASE PLANK – OFF HANDS (RIGHT)

Targeted Muscles: Abdominals, shoulders

Lying on your stomach, place your forearms and hands on the floor, with your elbows directly under your shoulders. Lift your body up off the floor using the pressure from your arms and toes. Tilt your tailbone toward the floor (as if you were slightly tucking your buttocks underneath you). This helps to isolate your abdominal muscles.

3. STAIRS

Targeted Muscles: Front and back of legs, buttocks, calves, your heart

Walk, jog or run up and down a flight of stairs. The objective is to pace yourself so you can maintain movement for the duration of the exercise, without stopping. Complete 2 minutes.

SERIES THREE
(Repeat the series once)

1. WALKING

Targeted Muscles: Front and back of legs, buttocks, your heart

Walk inside on a track, on a treadmill, or outside. The main objective is to increase your heart rate and maintain a continuous, moderate pace that will help build your muscular and cardiovascular endurance. Keep a brisk pace, one that would allow you to carry on a conversation with someone while still needing to periodically catch your breath. Walk for 15 minutes.

4:56
Beginner Workout Two

Warm-up		
Stairs or treadmill walk	5 mins	Light to moderate pace
Series One: Repeat the series twice		
1. Squats	15	Moderate weight
2. Alternating back lunges	10/side	Light weight
3. Stairs	3 mins	
4. Plank off elbows	30 secs	
Series Two: Repeat the series twice		
1. Lateral shuffles	1 min/side	
2. Stationary side lunge	12/side	Light weight
3. Jumping-jack planks	30	
Series Three: Repeat the series once		
1. Walking	30 mins	Moderate pace

SERIES ONE
(Repeat the series twice)

1. SQUATS

Targeted Muscles: Front and back of legs, buttocks
Stand with your feet shoulder-width apart (the insides of your feet should be in line with the outsides of your shoulders). Bend at your hips and knees to lower into a squat position (as if you're about to sit in a chair) until your thighs are just past parallel to the floor. If you have knee problems, do not go past parallel. Keep your knees over your ankles (you should be able to see your toes throughout the entire movement). Maintain good posture by keeping your chest up as you stand up, pushing through your heels. Complete 15 repetitions.

2. ALTERNATING BACK LUNGES

Targeted Muscles: Front and back of legs, buttocks

Take a large step back and bend both your knees to 90° so that your back knee almost touches the floor. Keep your front knee tracking over your ankle. Push through your front heel and stand up, placing both feet together. Repeat, moving back with the opposite leg. Complete 10 repetitions (alternating) on each side.

3. STAIRS

Targeted Muscles: Front and back of legs, buttocks, calves, your heart

Walk, jog or run up and down a flight of stairs. The objective is to pace yourself so you can maintain movement for the duration of the exercise, without stopping. Complete 3 minutes.

4. PLANK OFF ELBOWS

Targeted Muscles: Shoulders, abdominals

Lying on your stomach, place your forearms and hands on the floor, with your elbows directly under your shoulders. Lift your body up off the floor using the pressure from your arms and your toes. Tilt your tailbone toward the floor (as if you were slightly tucking your buttocks underneath you). This helps to isolate your abdominal muscles. Hold this position for 30 seconds.

SERIES TWO
(Repeat the series twice)

1. LATERAL SHUFFLES

Targeted Muscles: Sides of legs, buttocks, calves, your heart

You will need a long space like a hallway to perform this exercise, as you will be covering a little distance with each step to the side. From a standing position, take a lateral (sideways) step to the right with your right foot. Carry your left foot in to the spot where your right foot was. While pushing off with the left foot, take another lateral step with your right foot. Continue this pattern for 1 minute in the same direction, then repeat in the opposite direction (pushing off the opposite foot) for another minute. Think of this exercise as running sideways! Note: This exercise can also be performed on a treadmill. For safety, keep one hand on the treadmill handle and perform at a slow speed.

2. STATIONARY SIDE LUNGE

Targeted Muscles: Front, back and inner legs, buttocks

Take a large step to one side so that your feet are wider than shoulder-width apart. Keep both feet facing forward. On one side, slowly bend at the hip and push your body weight back onto your heel while you bend your knee, keeping your other leg straight. Push yourself back up into a standing position (using the bent leg). Note that your feet do not move during this exercise (hence "stationary"). Complete 12 repetitions on one side, then switch to the other side.

3. JUMPING-JACK PLANKS (RIGHT)

Targeted Muscles: Shoulders, abdominals, upper back, your heart

From a plank position off your hands (see Base Plank off Hands, page 123), quickly jump both feet simultaneously outward to shoulder-width apart, then back to centre. Complete 30 repetitions as quickly as you can.

SERIES THREE
(Repeat the series once)

1. WALKING

Targeted Muscles: Front and back of legs, buttocks, your heart

Walk inside on a track, on a treadmill, or outside. The main objective is to increase your heart rate and maintain a continuous, moderate pace that will help build your muscular and cardiovascular endurance. Keep a brisk pace, one that would allow you to carry on a conversation with someone while still needing to periodically catch your breath. Walk for 30 minutes

7/88
Beginner Workout Three

Warm-up		
Stairs or treadmill walk	5–10 mins	Light to moderate pace
Series One: Repeat the series twice		
1. Front squats	15	Light weight
2. Walking lunges	1 min	Light weight
3. Walkouts	10	
Series Two: Repeat the series twice		
1. Wide–narrow jump squats	15 each	
2. Glute bridge	1 min	
3. Single foot hops	25/side	
4. Push-ups off knees	10	
5. 3-point mid row	12/side	Moderate weight
Series Three: Repeat the series once		
1. Walking	30 mins	Moderate pace

SERIES ONE
(Repeat the series twice)

1. FRONT SQUATS

Targeted Muscles: Front and back of legs, buttocks, shoulders, abdominals

Stand with your feet shoulder-width apart. Holding a dumbbell in each hand, lift each weight up so that they are parallel to the floor and the ends are in line with the front of your shoulders. With your head and chest up, slowly bend at the hips and knees into a squat position. If you have knee problems, do not go past parallel. Keep your knees over your ankles (you should be able to see your toes throughout the entire movement). Keep the dumbbells close to your chest during the entire movement. Complete 15 repetitions.

2. WALKING LUNGES (OPPOSITE)

Targeted Muscles: Front, back and inner legs, buttocks, calves

Holding a dumbbell in each hand, arms at your sides, take one large step forward so that when you bend your knees they form two 90° angles. Keep your chest up during the entire exercise. Take another step forward and bend your knees once again to form two 90° angles. As you stand up from each lunge, be sure to push through your front heel to keep your front knee over your front ankle. Complete for 1 minute.

3. WALKOUTS

Targeted Muscles: Shoulders, abdominals, chest, upper back

Start in a standing position. Bend at the waist and place your hands on the floor (if necessary, bend your knees slightly). Once your hands are on the floor, slowly walk one hand out at a time until your back is parallel to the floor (a plank position with your hands located directly under your shoulders). Pause, then walk one hand at a time back toward your feet. Once you reach your feet, stand up. Complete 10 repetitions.

SERIES TWO
(Repeat the series twice)

1. WIDE–NARROW JUMP SQUATS

Targeted Muscles: Front, back and inner legs, buttocks, calves, your heart

Start in a wide squat position (see Squats, page 119), with feet farther than shoulder-width apart. From the squat, jump up into a narrow squat position, with both feet together. From the narrow squat position, jump back into a wide squat position. If you have knee problems, do not go past parallel. Keep your knees over your ankles (you should be able to see your toes throughout the entire movement). Keep your chest up during the entire movement. Repeat as quickly as you can for 15 repetitions of each.

2. GLUTE BRIDGE

Targeted Muscles: Buttocks, back of legs

Lie on the floor with your knees bent directly over your ankles, and with feet hip-width apart. Squeeze your glutes and slowly lift your hips off the floor, high enough to enhance the tension in your glutes without arching your lower back. Do not allow your knees to roll inward. Most of the pressure should be in the heels of your feet. Hold this position for 1 minute.

1   2   3   4

3. SINGLE FOOT HOPS

Targeted Muscles: Buttocks, front of legs, calves,
muscles of the feet
Stand on one foot and jump in place for 25 repetitions. Repeat on the other foot.

4. PUSH-UPS OFF KNEES

Targeted Muscles: Abdominals, upper back, chest, shoulders

Lie face down on the floor with your hands directly underneath your shoulders. Bend your knees, keeping your feet on the floor, as you raise your body up off the floor until your arms are straight. With a tight core (as if you were slightly tucking your buttocks underneath you), slowly lower your body down in a straight line, moving your shoulders and hips at the same rate. Your chest should fall between your hands. Go as low as you can without resting your body on the floor, pause, and then push yourself up to the starting position. Complete 10 repetitions.

5. 3-POINT MID ROW (LEFT)

Targeted Muscles: Front and back of arms, front and back of shoulders, mid-back, upper back

Holding a dumbbell in your right hand, rest your left hand on a platform, such as an exercise bench or a chair, for support. Keeping your back straight and your shoulders parallel to the floor, slowly pull the weight up toward the outside of your rib cage. Lower the weight down to your starting position. Complete 12 repetitions on each side of your body.

SERIES THREE
(Repeat the series once)

1. WALKING

Targeted Muscles: Front and back of legs, buttocks, your heart

Walk inside on a track, on a treadmill, or outside. The main objective is to increase your heart rate and maintain a continuous, moderate pace that will help build your muscular and cardiovascular endurance. Keep a brisk pace, one that would allow you to carry on a conversation with someone while still needing to periodically catch your breath. Walk for 30 minutes.

5895
Beginner Workout Four

Warm-up		
Stairs or treadmill walk	5–10 mins	Light to moderate pace
Series One: Repeat the series twice		
1. Goblet squats	20	Moderate weight
2. Back lunge with hop	12/side	
3. Low jacks	40	
Series Two: Repeat the series twice		
1. Lateral shuffles	1 min/side	
2. Calf raises	25/direction	Moderate weight
3. Single leg forward hops	10/side	
4. Glute bridge pulses	25	
5. Standing palms-in dumbbell press	12	Light weight
6. Lateral Raises	12	Light weight
Series Three: Repeat the series once		
1. Walking	30 mins	Moderate pace

SERIES ONE
(Repeat the series twice)

1. GOBLET SQUATS

Targeted Muscles: Front and back of legs, buttocks
Holding a dumbbell at one end with both hands (as if you were holding a large goblet), stand with your feet shoulder-width apart (the insides of your feet should be in line with the outsides of your shoulders). Maintain good posture by keeping your chest up as you bend at your hips and knees, lowering into a squat position (as if you're about to sit in a chair) until your thighs are just past parallel to the floor. If you have knee problems, do not go past parallel. Keep your knees over your ankles (you should be able to see your toes throughout the entire movement). Keep the dumbbell close to your chest during the entire movement. Stand back up, pushing through your heels. Complete 20 repetitions.

2. BACK LUNGE WITH HOP

Targeted Muscles: Front and back of legs, calves, buttocks

Take a large step backward into a lunge. Your back knee should be just an inch off the floor, and your front knee should track nicely over your ankle. Stand back up out of the lunge by pushing through your front heel. Swing your back leg forward and tuck your knee in toward your body, then hop on the balancing foot. Challenge your balance by jumping as high as you can and by not touching the ground during this transition. Complete 12 repetitions with one leg, and then repeat with the other leg.

3. LOW JACKS

Targeted Muscles: Front, back and inner legs, buttocks, calves, your heart

Start with your feet together and your knees slightly bent, hands on your hips. While maintaining this position, jump your feet out to shoulder-width apart, then jump back into your starting position. Repeat this in-and-out jumping pattern as quickly as you can for 40 repetitions.

SERIES TWO
(Repeat the series twice)

1. LATERAL SHUFFLES

Targeted Muscles: Sides of legs, buttocks, calves, your heart

You will need a long space like a hallway to perform this exercise, as you will be covering a little distance with each step to the side. From a standing position, take a lateral (sideways) step to the right with your right foot. Carry your left foot in to the spot where your right foot was. While pushing off with the left foot, take another lateral step with your right foot. Continue this pattern for 1 minute in the same direction, then repeat in the opposite direction (pushing off the opposite foot) for another minute. Think of this exercise as running sideways! Note: This exercise can also be performed on a treadmill. For safety, keep one hand on the treadmill handle and perform at a slow speed.

1　　3　　5

2. CALF RAISES (OPPOSITE, WITH CLOSEUP FOOT POSITIONS ABOVE)

Targeted Muscles: Calves, muscles of the feet, front of lower leg

Note that this is an exercise in three parts. Stand with your torso upright, holding a dumbbell in each hand, arms by your sides. With your toes pointing forward (targeting all aspects of the calves), raise your heels off the floor, contracting the muscles in your calves as you stand on your toes. Hold for 1–2 seconds at the top, then lower your feet back down. Complete 25 repetitions, then switch your foot position so that your toes point slightly inward (targeting the outer portion of your calves). Complete the 25 repetitions again and then switch your foot position once more, this time pointing your toes slightly outward (targeting the inner portion of your calves). Complete 25 repetitions one last time.

3. SINGLE LEG FORWARD HOPS

Targeted Muscles: Buttocks, front of legs, calves, muscles of the feet

Stand on one foot and jump as far forward as you can, without losing your balance. Pause and then jump again. Complete 10 repetitions, then repeat on the other foot.

4. GLUTE BRIDGE PULSES

Targeted Muscles: Buttocks, back of legs

Lie on the floor with your knees bent directly over your ankles, and with feet hip-width apart. Squeeze your glutes and slowly lift your hips off the floor, high enough to enhance the tension in your glutes without arching your lower back. Do not allow your knees to roll inward. Most of the pressure should be in the heels of your feet as you hold this position for 1–2 seconds at the top. Lower your hips without resting them on the floor. Remember to squeeze your glutes before lifting your hips upward for each. Complete 25 repetitions.

5. STANDING PALMS-IN DUMBBELL PRESS

Targeted Muscles: Shoulders, abdominals

Stand with your feet shoulder-width apart and your knees slightly bent. Holding a dumbbell in each hand, lift the weights to shoulder height, keeping your palms facing in toward each other. Slowly and simultaneously push the dumbbells upward until your arms are fully extended over your shoulders, then lower your arms back down to your starting position. Complete 12 repetitions.

6. LATERAL RAISES (LEFT)

Targeted Muscles: Sides of shoulders, upper back

With a dumbbell in each hand and tall posture, slowly raise both arms up to your sides, no higher than shoulder height. Keep your shoulder blades down your back. (You know you are in the correct position if you start the exercise by lifting your shoulders up, back and down. This is called the shoulder set position.) Pause with the dumbbells at your sides for 1 second before slowly lowering the weights down. Complete 12 repetitions.

SERIES THREE
(Repeat the series once)

1. WALKING

Targeted Muscles: Front and back of legs, buttocks, your heart

Walk inside on a track, on a treadmill, or outside. The main objective is to increase your heart rate and maintain a continuous, moderate pace that will help build your muscular and cardiovascular endurance. Keep a brisk pace, one that would allow you to carry on a conversation with someone while still needing to periodically catch your breath. Walk for 30 minutes.

MACHAME
Intermediate Workout One

Warm-up		
Foam roller	See Appendix A	
Treadmill incline walk	5–10 mins	Moderate pace
Series One: Repeat the series three times		
1. Goblet squats	20	Moderate weight
2. Jump squats	15	
3. Calf raises	25/direction	Moderate weight
4. Mini-band lateral walk	12/side	Medium to heavy weight band
Series Two: Repeat the series three times		
1. Low jacks	40	
2. Sliding towel hillclimbers	30 secs	
3. Back lunge with knee tuck	12/side	Moderate weight
Series Three: Repeat the series three times		
1. Bench press off floor	15	Moderate weight
2. Walkout with push-up	8	

SERIES ONE
(Repeat the series three times)

1. GOBLET SQUATS

Targeted Muscles: Front and back of legs, buttocks

Holding a dumbbell at one end with both hands (as if you were holding a large goblet), stand with your feet shoulder-width apart (the insides of your feet should be in line with the outsides of your shoulders). Maintain good posture by keeping your chest up as you bend at your hips and knees, lowering into a squat position (as if you're about to sit in a chair) until your thighs are just past parallel to the floor. If you have knee problems, do not go past parallel. Keep your knees over your ankles (you should be able to see your toes throughout the entire movement). Keep the dumbbell close to your chest during the entire movement. Stand back up, pushing through your heels. Complete 20 repetitions.

2. JUMP SQUATS (LEFT)

Targeted Muscles: Front and back of legs, buttocks, abdominals, your heart

Start in a base squat position (see Squats, page 119). Bend down into a squat (keeping your knees over your ankles and your chest up) and leap from this position up off the floor, catching yourself in another squat as you come down. Complete 15 repetitions.

3. CALF RAISES (OPPOSITE, SEE ALSO CLOSEUP FOOT POSITION PHOTO ON PAGE 147)

Targeted Muscles: Calves, muscles of the feet, front of lower leg

Note that this is an exercise in three parts. Stand with your torso upright, holding a dumbbell in each hand, arms by your sides. With your toes pointing forward (targeting all aspects of the calves), raise your heels off the floor, contracting the muscles in your calves as you stand on your toes. Hold for 1–2 seconds at the top, then lower your feet back down. Complete 25 repetitions, then switch your foot position so that your toes point slightly inward (targeting the outer portion of your calves). Complete 25 repetitions again and then switch your foot position once more, this time pointing your toes slightly outward (targeting the inner portion of your calves). Complete 25 repetitions one last time.

4. MINI-BAND LATERAL WALK (ABOVE)

Targeted Muscles: Buttocks (in particular, side of buttocks)

Place a mini-band around your lower legs, midcalves. If you place the band closer to the knees, the tension is less than if you place it lower, around the ankles. With the band in place, feet shoulder-width apart and your chest up, slowly step laterally in one direction for 12 steps. Maintain a shoulder-width stance so the band has tension in it throughout the exercise and does not slip. Repeat, moving 12 steps in the opposite direction, leading with the opposite leg.

SERIES TWO
(Repeat the series three times)

1. LOW JACKS (OPPOSITE)

Targeted Muscles: Front, back and inner legs, buttocks, calves, your heart

Start with your feet together and your knees slightly bent, hands on your hips. While maintaining this position, jump your feet out to shoulder-width apart, then jump back into your starting position. Repeat this in-and-out jumping pattern as quickly as you can for 40 repetitions.

2. SLIDING TOWEL HILLCLIMBERS (ABOVE)

Targeted Muscles: Shoulders, abdominals, chest, hip flexors, your heart

On a smooth surface, take two small towels and place one under each of your feet. Take a plank position off your hands (see Base Plank off Hands, page 123). Tighten your core and then crunch your right knee up toward your chest, gliding your foot along the floor with the help of the towel. After your right knee reaches your chest, push your foot back along the floor. Repeat the same gliding movement with your left leg. Keep your hips parallel to floor during the entire exercise. The less the hips move, the more impact the exercise has. This movement should be done as quickly as possible, while maintaining good form, to elevate your heart rate. Complete this alternating movement for 30 seconds.

3. BACK LUNGE WITH KNEE TUCK
(OPPOSITE)

Targeted Muscles: Front and back of legs, calves, buttocks, abdominals

Holding a dumbbell in each hand, arms at your sides, take a large step backward into a lunge. Your back knee should be just an inch off the floor, and your front knee should track nicely over your ankle. Stand back up out of the lunge by pushing through your front heel. Swing your back leg forward and tuck your knee in toward your body, then step back into the lunge. Challenge your balance by not touching the ground during this transition. Complete 12 repetitions with one leg, and then repeat with the other leg.

1

2

3

SERIES THREE
(Repeat the series three times)

1. BENCH PRESS OFF FLOOR (LEFT)
Targeted Muscles: Front and back of arms, shoulders, chest

With a dumbbell in each hand, lie on your back with your knees bent and feet flat on the floor. Start with both weights above your chest, your arms extended. Slowly and simultaneously lower both weights down to your sides to a 90° angle in your arms (your wrists should track over your elbows as you lower the weights). Lower your arms as far as possible without resting your elbows on the floor. Pause at the bottom for one second, then press the weights back up to the starting position. Complete 15 repetitions.

2. WALKOUT WITH PUSH-UP (OPPOSITE)
Targeted Muscles: Shoulders, abdominals, chest, upper back

Start in a standing position. Bend at the waist and place your hands on the floor (if necessary, bend your knees slightly). Once your hands are on the floor, slowly walk one hand out at a time until your back is parallel to the floor (a plank position, with your hands located directly under your shoulders). Pause, then perform one push-up (see Push-ups, page 204). Walk one hand at a time back toward your feet. Once you reach your feet, stand up. Complete 8 repetitions.

Umbwe: Intermediate Workout Two

Warm-up		
Foam roller	See Appendix A	
Treadmill incline walk	5–10 mins	Moderate pace
Series One: Repeat the series three times		
1. Squat with single arm press	12/side	Moderate weight
2. Single leg lunges	12/side	Moderate weight
3. Lateral lunges (dynamic)	12/side	Moderate weight
Series Two: Repeat the series three times		
1. Lawnmower	12/side	Moderate weight
2. Rear delt flys	12	Light weight
3. Plank off ball	45 secs	
Series Three: Repeat the series three times		
1. Glute bridge pulses	1 min	Moderate weight
2. Mini-band jacks	20	Medium to heavy weight band

SERIES ONE
(Repeat the series three times)

1. SQUAT WITH SINGLE ARM PRESS
Targeted Muscles: Front and back of legs, buttocks, shoulders, abdominals

Stand with your feet shoulder-width apart. Holding a dumbbell in one hand, lift the weight up so that it is parallel to the floor and the end is in line with the front of your shoulder. Bend your hips and knees into a squat position (see Squats, page 119). Keep your knees behind your toes and your chest up. As you push through your heels to stand up, slowly push the dumbbell upward over your head. Bring the weight back down to the front of your shoulder. Complete 12 repetitions on each side.

2. SINGLE LEG LUNGES (LEFT)

Targeted Muscles: Front and back of legs, buttocks, abdominals

Holding a dumbbell in each hand, arms at your sides, step back with one leg and place the top of your foot on an elevated and stable surface (a bench, chair, stair). Take a large step forward with your other leg. Bend your front knee until your thigh is parallel to the floor, and then stand back up by pushing through the heel of your balancing/ front foot. Keep your knee tracking over your ankle rather than over your front toe. Complete 12 repetitions, then switch to the other leg.

3. LATERAL LUNGES – DYNAMIC (OPPOSITE)

Targeted Muscles: Front, back and inner legs, calves, buttocks, abdominals, upper back, shoulders

Holding a dumbbell at one end with both hands, take a large step to one side so that your feet are wider than shoulder-width apart. Keep your toes pointing forward. On one side, slowly bend at the hip and push your body weight back onto your heel while you bend your knee, keeping your other leg straight. Then, push yourself back up into a standing position (using the bent leg) so that your feet meet back in the middle. Keep the dumbbell close to your chest during the entire movement. Complete 12 repetitions on one side, then switch to the other side.

SERIES TWO
(Repeat the series three times)

1. LAWNMOWER

Targeted Muscles: Front, back and inner legs, front and back of arms, front and back of shoulders, buttocks, mid-back, side of torso

From standing, and with a dumbbell on the floor in front of you, take a large step to one side so that your feet are wider than shoulder-width apart. Keep your toes pointing forward. Leaning to your right side, slowly bend at your right hip, pushing your body weight back onto your heel while you bend the right knee. Keep your left leg straight (See Stationary Side Lunge position, page 129). Rest your right elbow on your bent right knee. With the left hand, grab the dumbbell and hold it beneath you. From here, pull the weight upward in the direction of your rib cage and rotate your torso (mimicking the motion of pulling a lawnmower cord). Be sure your head turns in the same direction as your arm to protect your neck from kinking. Each pull is one repetition. Complete 12 repetitions on the right side (with left arm pulling), then switch and repeat with your left leg (right arm pulling).

2. REAR DELT FLYS

Targeted Muscles: Upper back, back of shoulders

Holding a dumbbell in each hand, arms at your sides and palms facing thighs, bend at the hips and slightly in the knees, maintaining a straight/flat back. Slowly raise your arms out up your sides to shoulder height, with your elbows slightly bent. It is important that you can see the weights in your peripheral vision so you know you are not raising them too far behind you. Pause at shoulder height for 1 second, and then lower both arms back down below your chest. Complete 12 repetitions.

3. PLANK OFF BALL

Targeted Muscles: Upper back, shoulders, abdominals

Place both elbows directly underneath your shoulders onto an exercise ball. Extend one leg out at a time to form a plank position. With a tight core (tilt your tailbone toward the floor), hold this position for 45 seconds.

SERIES THREE
(Repeat the series three times)

1. GLUTE BRIDGE PULSES

Targeted Muscles: Buttocks, back of legs

Lie on the floor with your knees bent directly over your ankles, and with feet hip-width apart. Place a dumbbell directly over the crease of your hips and hold it in place with your hands to prevent it from rolling as you perform the exercise. Squeeze your glutes and slowly lift your hips off the floor, high enough to enhance the tension in your glutes without arching your lower back. Your back should remain straight and in line with your hips. Do not allow your knees to roll inward. Most of the pressure should be in the heels of your feet as you hold this position for 1–2 seconds at the top. Lower your hips without resting them on the floor. Remember to squeeze your glutes before lifting your hips upward for each pulse. Complete this movement for 1 minute.

2. MINI-BAND JACKS

Targeted Muscles: Buttocks (in particular, side of buttocks), calves

Place a mini-band around your lower legs, mid-calves. If you place the band closer to the knees, the tension is less than if you place it lower, around the ankles. With the band in place, feet shoulder-width apart and your chest up, jump your feet out slightly farther than shoulder-width apart, then jump back in just far enough that the band still has tension. Repeat this in-and-out jumping movement for 20 repetitions.

MARANGU
Intermediate Workout Three

Warm-up		
Foam roller	See Appendix A	
Treadmill incline walk	10 mins	Incline 15, moderate pace
Series One: Repeat the series four times		
1. Squats	30 secs	Moderate weight
2. Burpees	30 secs	
3. Single foot hops	30 secs/side	
4. Alternating back lunges	1 min	Moderate weight
5. Walkouts	30 secs	
6. Standing palms-in dumbbell press	30 secs	Light weight
7. Low jacks	30 secs	
8. Side-to-side jump lunges	30 secs	
9. Stairs	1 min	

SERIES ONE
(Repeat the series four times)

1. SQUATS (ABOVE)

Targeted Muscles: Front and back of legs, buttocks

Holding a dumbbell in each hand, arms at your sides, stand with your feet shoulder-width apart (the insides of your feet should be in line with the outsides of your shoulders). Bend at your hips and knees to lower into a squat position (as if you're about to sit in a chair) until your thighs are just past parallel to the floor. If you have knee problems, do not go past parallel. Keep your knees over your ankles (you should be able to see your toes throughout the entire movement). Maintain good posture by keeping your chest up as you stand up, pushing through your heels. Complete as many repetitions as you can in 30 seconds.

2. BURPEES (OPPOSITE)

Targeted Muscles: Front and back of legs, upper back, shoulders, abdominals, chest, your heart

Place your hands on the floor. Jump both feet back simultaneously into a plank position, then jump both feet back up simultaneously to a deep squat position. Stand up and jump. This is one repetition. Complete as many repetitions as you can in 30 seconds.

3. SINGLE FOOT HOPS

Targeted Muscles: Buttocks, front of legs, calves,
muscles of the feet

Stand on one foot and jump in place for 30 seconds.

Repeat on the other foot.

4. ALTERNATING BACK LUNGES

Targeted Muscles: Front and back of legs, buttocks

Holding a dumbbell in each hand, arms at your sides, take a large step back and bend both of your knees to 90° so that your back knee almost touches the floor. Keep your front knee tracking over your ankle. Push through your front heel and stand up, placing both feet together. Repeat, moving back with the opposite leg. Repeat this alternating movement for 1 minute.

5. WALKOUTS

Targeted Muscles: Shoulders, abdominals, chest, upper back

Start in a standing position. Bend at the waist and place your hands on the floor (if necessary, bend your knees slightly). Once your hands are on the floor, slowly walk one hand out at a time until your back is parallel to the floor (a plank position, with your hands located directly under your shoulders). Pause, then walk one hand at a time back toward your feet. Once you reach your feet, stand up. Complete as many repetitions as you can in 30 seconds.

6. STANDING PALMS-IN DUMBBELL PRESS
(ABOVE)

Targeted Muscles: Shoulders, abdominals

Stand with your feet shoulder-width apart and your knees slightly bent. Holding a dumbbell in each hand, lift the weights to shoulder height, keeping your palms facing in toward each other. Slowly and simultaneously push the dumbbells upward until your arms are fully extended over your shoulders, then lower your arms back down to your starting position. Repeat for 30 seconds.

7. LOW JACKS (OPPOSITE)

Targeted Muscles: Front, back and inner legs, buttocks, calves, your heart

Start with your feet together and your knees slightly bent, hands on your hips. While maintaining this position, jump your feet out to shoulder-width apart, then jump back into your starting position. Repeat this in-and-out jumping pattern as quickly as you can for 30 seconds.

8. SIDE-TO-SIDE JUMP LUNGES (ABOVE)

Targeted Muscles: Front, back and inner legs, buttocks, abdominals, your heart

From a standing position, take a large step to one side so that your feet are wider than shoulder-width apart. Keep your toes pointing forward. Slowly bend at the hip and push your body weight back onto your heel while you bend one knee. Keep your other leg straight. Pushing from your bent leg, jump yourself back up to centre and land in another side lunge on the opposite leg. Repeat this side-to-side movement for 30 seconds.

9. STAIRS

Targeted Muscles: Front and back of legs, buttocks, calves, your heart

Jog or run up and down a flight of stairs. Maintain your fastest pace, without stopping, for 1 minute.

Shira: Intermediate Workout Four

Warm-up		
Foam roller	See Appendix A	
Treadmill incline walk	5–10 mins	Incline 15, moderate pace
Series One: Repeat the series three times		
1. Squats with mini-band	25	Medium band
2. Toe touches	15/side	
3. Hamstring curls off ball	20	
Series Two: Repeat the series three times		
1. Single leg lateral raises	10/side	Light weight
2. Single leg forward hops	30 secs/side	
Series Three: Repeat the series three times		
1. Kneeling single arm shoulder press	12/side	Moderate weight
2. Alternating mid row	15/side	Moderate weight
3. Salamanders	15/side	
Series Four: Repeat the series twice		
1. Lateral shuffles	1 min/side	

SERIES ONE
(Repeat the series three times)

1. SQUATS WITH MINI-BAND

Targeted Muscles: Front and back of legs, buttocks

Place a mini-band around both thighs, just above your knees. Start with your feet shoulder-width apart. Push your knees outward slightly toward the mini-band to prevent them from caving inward. Bend your hips and knees to lower into a squat position (see Squats, page 119). Maintain good posture by keeping your chest up as you lower into the squat and while you stand back up, pushing through your heels. Complete 25 repetitions.

2. TOE TOUCHES

Targeted Muscles: Front and back of legs, buttocks, calves

Stand on one foot, with your other leg bent behind you at approximately 90°. Slowly bend your standing leg at the knee and then bend forward at the hip to reach for the floor with both hands while maintaining a flat back. Gently touch the floor, and then slowly stand up. Complete 15 repetitions on one leg, and then repeat with the other leg.

3. HAMSTRING CURLS OFF BALL

Targeted Muscles: Back of legs, calves, buttocks, abdominals

Lie on your back and place your heels top and centre on an exercise ball. Flex your feet (point your toes to the ceiling) and elevate your hips off the floor. Avoid arching your back by engaging your abdominal and buttocks muscles. Once in this position, slowly push your heels into the ball and drag it inward to your buttocks. Pause, then push the ball out with your feet, keeping your hips up the entire time. Complete 20 repetitions.

SERIES TWO
(Repeat the series three times)

1. SINGLE LEG LATERAL RAISES
Targeted Muscles: Side of shoulders, front and back of legs, abdominals, upper back, buttocks, calves

With a dumbbell in each hand and tall posture, balance on one foot with your other leg at 90° in front of you. Slowly raise both arms up to your sides, no higher than shoulder height. Keep your shoulder blades down your back. (You know you are in the correct position if you start the exercise by lifting your shoulders up, back and down. This is called the shoulder set position.) Pause with the dumbbells at your sides for 1 second before slowly lowering the weights down. Complete 10 repetitions on one side, and then repeat on the other leg.

2. SINGLE LEG FORWARD HOPS (OPPOSITE)

Targeted Muscles: Buttocks, front of legs, calves, muscles of the feet

Stand on one foot and jump as far forward as you can, without losing your balance. Pause and then jump again. Continue hopping forward for 30 seconds, then repeat on the other foot.

SERIES THREE
(Repeat the series three times)

1. KNEELING SINGLE ARM
SHOULDER PRESS (RIGHT)

Targeted Muscles: Shoulders, abdominals, side of torso, buttocks

Kneel on your right knee and hold a dumbbell in your right hand with your arm at 90°. From this position, slowly press the dumbbell up, and then lower your arm back down to 90°. Maintain an upright position with your torso. Complete 12 repetitions on the right side, then repeat on the left knee, with the left arm.

2. ALTERNATING MID ROW

Targeted Muscles: Upper back, front and back of arms, shoulders, abdominals

Holding a dumbbell in each hand, arms at your sides, stand with your feet shoulder-width apart. Bend your knees slightly and flex your torso forward, keeping your back flat. Squeeze your buttocks to maintain a strong core, and keep your weight in your heels. Slowly bring one dumbbell up and down at a time (alternating) toward your rib cage. Complete 15 repetitions per side.

3. SALAMANDERS

Targeted Muscles: Shoulders, abdominals, chest, side of torso

Start in a plank position off your hands (see Base Plank off Hands, page 123). With a tight core, crunch your right knee up to the outside of your right elbow, turning your head in the direction of your bending knee to enhance the crunch. Step the leg back, then repeat the crunch with your left knee to your left elbow. Complete this alternating movement for 15 repetitions on each side.

SERIES FOUR
(Repeat the series twice)

1. LATERAL SHUFFLES

Targeted Muscles: Sides of legs, buttocks, calves, your heart

You will need a long space like a hallway to perform this exercise, as you will be covering a little distance with each step to the side. From a standing position, take a lateral (sideways) step to the right with your right foot. Carry your left foot in to the spot where your right foot was. While pushing off with the left foot, take another lateral step with your right foot. Continue this pattern for 1 minute in the same direction, then repeat in the opposite direction (pushing off the opposite foot) for another minute. Think of this exercise as running sideways! Note: This exercise can also be performed on a treadmill. For safety, keep one hand on the treadmill handle and perform at a slow speed.

RONGAI
Intermediate Workout Five

Warm-up		
Foam roller	See Appendix A	
Treadmill incline walk	5 mins	Incline 15, moderate pace
Series One: Repeat the series three times		
1. Front squats	20	Moderate weight
2. Alternating back lunges	12/side	Moderate weight
3. Glute bridge	1 min	Moderate weight
4. Calf raises	20 secs/direction	
Series Two: Repeat the series three times		
1. Alternating bench press	15/side	Moderate weight
2. Supermans	15	
3. Alternating mid row	15/side	Moderate weight
Series Three: Repeat the series three times		
1. Side plank off feet	30 secs/side	
2. Half burpees	15	
3. Plank off elbows	45 secs	

SERIES ONE
(Repeat the series three times)

1. FRONT SQUATS

Targeted Muscles: Front and back of legs, buttocks, shoulders, abdominals

Stand with your feet shoulder-width apart. Holding a dumbbell in each hand, lift each weight up so that they are parallel to the floor and the ends are in line with the front of your shoulders. With your head and chest up, slowly bend at the hips and knees into a squat position. If you have knee problems, do not go past parallel. Keep your knees over your ankles (you should be able to see your toes throughout the entire movement). Keep the dumbbells close to your chest during the entire movement. Stand up by pushing through your heels. Complete 20 repetitions.

2. ALTERNATING BACK LUNGES

Targeted Muscles: Front and back of legs, buttocks

Holding a dumbbell in each hand, arms at your sides, take a large step back and bend both of your knees to 90° so that your back knee almost touches the floor. Keep your front knee tracking over your ankle. Push through your front heel and stand up, placing both feet together. Repeat, moving back with the opposite leg. Complete 12 repetitions per side.

3. GLUTE BRIDGE (BELOW)

Targeted Muscles: Buttocks, back of legs

Lie on the floor with your knees bent directly over your ankles, and with feet hip-width apart. Place a dumbbell directly over the crease of your hips and hold it in place with your hands to prevent it from rolling as you perform the exercise. Squeeze your glutes and slowly lift your hips off the floor high enough to enhance the tension in your glutes without arching your lower back. Do not allow your knees to roll inward as you hold this position. Most of the pressure should be in the heels of your feet as you hold this position for 1 minute.

4. CALF RAISES (OPPOSITE, SEE ALSO CLOSEUP FOOT POSITION PHOTO ON PAGE 147)

Targeted Muscles: Calves, muscles of the feet, front of lower leg

Note that this is an exercise in three parts. Stand with your torso upright, arms by your sides. With your toes pointing forward (targeting all aspects of the calves), raise your heels off the floor, contracting the muscles in your calves as you stand on your toes and then lower your feet back down. Continue the up-down movement as quickly as you can for 20 seconds, then switch your foot position so that your toes point slightly inward (targeting the outer portion of your calves). Complete 20 seconds again and then switch your foot position once more, this time pointing your toes slightly outward (targeting the inner portion of your calves). Complete 20 seconds once more.

SERIES TWO
(Repeat the series three times)

1. ALTERNATING BENCH PRESS

Targeted Muscles: Front and backs of arms, shoulders, chest

With a dumbbell in each hand, lie on your back with your knees bent and feet flat on the floor. Start with arms extended, both weights above your chest, palms facing forward. Slowly lower your right arm, maintaining a 90° angle (your wrist should track over your elbow). Lower your arm as far as possible without resting your elbow on the floor. Pause at the bottom for 1 second, then press the weight back up to the starting position. Perform the same movement with the left arm. Complete 15 repetitions with each arm.

2. SUPERMANS

Targeted Muscles: Lower back, buttocks

Lie face down on the floor with your arms fully extended above your head. Simultaneously raise your arms, legs and chest off the floor and hold for 1–2 seconds. Squeeze your lower back and buttocks at the top of the movement. Slowly lower your arms, legs and chest back to the starting position. Complete 15 repetitions.

3. ALTERNATING MID ROW

Targeted Muscles: Upper back, front and back of arms, shoulders, abdominals

Holding a dumbbell in each hand, arms at your sides, stand with your feet shoulder-width apart. Bend your knees slightly and flex your torso forward, keeping your back flat. Squeeze your buttocks to maintain a strong core, and keep your weight in your heels. Slowly bring one dumbbell up and down at a time (alternating) toward your rib cage. Complete 15 repetitions per side.

SERIES THREE
(Repeat series three times)

1. SIDE PLANK OFF FEET

Targeted Muscles: Side of torso, upper back, shoulders

Lie on your side and extend your legs outward. Your feet, hips and shoulders should be in a straight line. Place your bottom elbow directly underneath your shoulder. Keep your bottom hand on the floor, perpendicular to your body. Using your oblique muscles (the sides of your torso) and a little pressure from your balancing elbow and the side of your foot, slowly raise your body weight up and lift your hips off the floor. Extend your top arm straight up so that your shoulders are in line, forming a T position with your body. Hold this position for 30 seconds, then repeat on the other side.

2. HALF BURPEES

Targeted Muscles: Front and back of legs, upper back, shoulders, abdominals, chest, your heart

Place your hands on the floor. Jump both feet back simultaneously into a plank position, then jump both feet back up simultaneously to a deep squat position. This is one repetition. Complete 15 repetitions.

3. PLANK OFF ELBOWS

Targeted Muscles: Abdominals, shoulders

Lying on your stomach, place your forearms and hands on the floor, with your elbows directly under your shoulders. Lift your body up off the floor using the pressure from your arms and your toes. Tilt your tailbone toward the floor (as if you were slightly tucking your buttocks underneath you). This helps to isolate your abdominal muscles. Hold this position for 45 seconds.

LEMOSHO
Intermediate Workout Six

Warm-up		
Foam roller	See Appendix A	
Treadmill incline walk	10 mins	Incline 15, moderate pace
Series One: Repeat the series four times		
1. Lateral shuffles	1 min/side	
2. Push-ups	30 secs	
3. Mini-band lateral walk	30 secs/side	Medium to heavy weight band
4. Goblet squats	30 secs	Moderate weight
5. Jump squats	30 secs	
6. Back lunge with knee tuck	30 secs/side	Moderate weight
7. Double stairs	1 min	
8. Single stairs	1 min	

SERIES ONE
(Repeat the series four times)

1. LATERAL SHUFFLES (OPPOSITE)

Targeted Muscles: Sides of legs, buttocks, calves, your heart

You will need a long space like a hallway to perform this exercise, as you will be covering a little distance with each step to the side. From a standing position, take a lateral (sideways) step to the right with your right foot. Carry your left foot in to the spot where your right foot was. While pushing off with the left foot, take another lateral step with your right foot. Continue this pattern for 1 minute in the same direction, then repeat in the opposite direction (pushing off the opposite foot) for another minute. Think of this exercise as running sideways!

Note: This exercise can also be performed on a treadmill. For safety, keep one hand on the treadmill handle and perform at a slow speed.

2. PUSH-UPS

Targeted Muscles: Abdominals, upper back, chest, shoulders

Start in a plank position off your toes with your hands directly underneath your shoulders. With a tight core (as if you were slightly tucking your buttocks underneath you), slowly lower your body down in a straight line, moving your shoulders and hips at the same rate. Your chest should fall between your hands. Go as low as you can without resting your body on the floor, pause, and then push yourself back up to the starting position. Repeat for 30 seconds.

3. MINI-BAND LATERAL WALK

Targeted Muscles: Buttocks (in particular, side of buttocks)

Place a mini-band around your lower legs, mid calves. If you place the band closer to the knees, the tension is less than if you place it lower, around the ankles. With the band in place, feet shoulder-width apart and your chest up, slowly step laterally in one direction for 30 seconds. Maintain a shoulder-width stance so the band has tension in it throughout the exercise and does not slip. Repeat moving in the opposite direction, leading with the opposite leg for another 30 seconds.

4. GOBLET SQUATS

Targeted Muscles: Front and back of legs, buttocks

Holding a dumbbell at one end with both hands (as if you were holding a large goblet), stand with your feet shoulder-width apart (the insides of your feet should be in line with the outsides of your shoulders). Maintain good posture by keeping your chest up as you bend at your hips and knees, lowering into a squat position (as if you're about to sit in a chair) until your thighs are just past parallel to the floor. If you have knee problems, do not go past parallel. Keep your knees over your ankles (you should be able to see your toes throughout the entire movement). Keep the dumbbell close to your chest during the entire movement. Stand back up, pushing through your heels. Repeat for 30 seconds.

5. JUMP SQUATS

Targeted Muscles: Front and back of legs, buttocks, abdominals, your heart

Start in a base squat position (see Squats, page 119). Bend down into a squat (keeping your knees over your ankles and your chest up) and leap from this position up off the floor, catching yourself in another squat as you come down. Repeat for 30 seconds.

6. BACK LUNGE WITH KNEE TUCK
(OPPOSITE)

Targeted Muscles: Front and back of legs, calves, buttocks, abdominals

Holding a dumbbell in each hand, arms at your sides, take a large step backward into a lunge. Your back knee should be just an inch off the floor, and your front knee should track nicely over your ankle. Stand back up out of the lunge by pushing through your front heel. Swing your back leg forward and tuck your knee in toward your body, then step back into the lunge. Challenge your balance by not touching the ground during this transition. Complete for 30 seconds with one leg, and then repeat with the other leg.

7. DOUBLE STAIRS

Targeted Muscles: Front and back of legs, buttocks, calves, your heart

Jog or run up a flight of stairs, taking them two stairs at a time (double). On the way down, take the stairs one stair at a time for safety. Maintain your fastest pace, without stopping, for 1 minute.

8. SINGLE STAIRS

Targeted Muscles: Front and back of legs, buttocks, calves, your heart

Walk, jog or run up and down a flight of stairs (one stair at a time). Maintain your fastest pace, without stopping, for 1 minute.

CHAGGA
Advanced Workout One

Warm-up		
Foam roller	See Appendix A	
Treadmill incline walk	10 mins	With backpack (10 lb) Incline 15, moderate pace
Series One: Repeat the series four times		
1. Front squats	20	Moderate weight
2. Glute bridge pulses	25	Moderate weight
3. Mini-band lateral walk	20 steps/side	Heavy weight band
Series Two: Repeat the series four times		
1. Jump squats	15	
2. Half burpees	15	
Series Three: Repeat the series three times		
1. Plank off ball with press-outs	1 min	
2. Push-ups with alternating rotations	8/side	
3. 3-point mid row	12/side	Moderate to heavy weight
4. Rear delt flys	15	Light to moderate weight

SERIES ONE
(Repeat the series four times)

1. FRONT SQUATS

Targeted Muscles: Front and back of legs, buttocks, shoulders, abdominals

Stand with your feet shoulder-width apart. Holding a dumbbell in each hand, lift each weight up so that they are parallel to the floor and the ends are in line with the front of your shoulders. With your head and chest up, slowly bend at the hips and knees into a squat position. If you have knee problems, do not go past parallel. Keep your knees over your ankles (you should be able to see your toes throughout the entire movement). Keep the dumbbells close to your chest during the entire movement. Stand up by pushing through your heels. Complete 20 repetitions.

2. GLUTE BRIDGE PULSES

Targeted Muscles: Buttocks, back of legs

Lie on the floor with your knees bent directly over your ankles, and with feet hip-width apart. Place a dumbbell directly over the crease of your hips and hold it in place with your hands to prevent it from rolling as you perform this exercise. Squeeze your glutes and slowly lift your hips off the floor, high enough to enhance the tension in your glutes without arching your lower back. Do not allow your knees to roll inward. Most of the pressure should be in the heels of your feet as you hold this position for 1–2 seconds at the top. Lower your hips without resting them on the floor. Remember to squeeze your glutes before lifting your hips upward for each pulse. Complete 25 repetitions.

3. MINI-BAND LATERAL WALK

Targeted Muscles: Buttocks (in particular, side of buttocks)

Place a mini-band around your lower legs, mid-calves. If you place the band closer to the knees, the tension is less than if you place it lower, around the ankles. With the band in place, feet shoulder-width apart and your chest up, slowly step laterally in one direction for 20 steps. Maintain a shoulder-width stance so the band has tension in it throughout the exercise and does not slip. Repeat, moving 20 steps in the opposite direction, leading with the opposite leg.

SERIES TWO
(Repeat the series four times)

1. JUMP SQUATS

Targeted Muscles: Front and back of legs, buttocks, abdominals, your heart

Start in a base squat position (see Squats, page 119). Bend down into a squat (keeping your knees over your ankles and your chest up) and leap from this position up off the floor, catching yourself in another squat as you come down. Complete 15 repetitions.

2. HALF BURPEES

Targeted Muscles: Front and back of legs, upper back, shoulders, abdominals, chest, your heart

Place your hands on the floor. Jump both feet back simultaneously into a plank position, then jump both feet back up simultaneously to a deep squat position. This is one repetition. Complete 15 repetitions.

SERIES THREE
(Repeat the series three times)

1. PLANK OFF BALL WITH PRESS-OUTS

Targeted Muscles: Upper back, shoulders, abdominals

Place both of your elbows directly underneath your shoulders onto an exercise ball. Extend one leg out at a time to form a plank position. With a tight core (tilt your tailbone toward the floor), slowly push the ball forward and back 2–3 inches underneath your body weight. Keep your body as still as possible as you move your arms. Continue this motion back and forth for 1 minute.

2. PUSH-UPS WITH ALTERNATING ROTATIONS (OPPOSITE)

Targeted Muscles: Abdominals, upper back, chest, shoulders

Start in a plank position off your toes with your hands directly underneath your shoulders. With a tight core (as if you were slightly tucking your buttocks underneath you), slowly lower your body down in a straight line, moving your shoulders and hips at the same rate. Your chest should fall between your hands. Go as low as you can without resting your body on the floor, pause, and then push yourself back up to the starting position. Once you reach the plank position, slowly raise your right hand off the floor and, maintaining a straight arm, rotate your torso until your arm is vertical, your body forming a T with your balancing arm. Slowly rotate down to the plank position and repeat the push-up with rotation on the other arm. Each push-up with one rotation is a repetition on that side. Complete 8 repetitions per side.

3. 3-POINT MID ROW

Targeted Muscles: Front and back of arms, front and back of shoulders, mid-back, upper back

Holding a dumbbell in your right hand, rest your left hand on a platform, such as an exercise bench or a chair, for support. Keeping your back straight and your shoulders parallel to the floor, slowly pull the weight up toward the outside of your rib cage. Lower the weight down to your starting position. Complete 12 repetitions per side.

4. REAR DELT FLYS

Targeted Muscles: Upper back, back of shoulders

Holding a dumbbell in each hand, arms at your sides and palms facing thighs, bend at the hips and slightly in the knees, maintaining a straight/flat back. Slowly raise your arms out up your sides to shoulder height, with your elbows slightly bent. It is important that you can see the weights in your peripheral vision so you know you are not raising them too far behind you. Pause at shoulder height for 1 second, and then lower both arms back down below your chest. Complete 15 repetitions.

MAASAI
Advanced Workout Two

Warm-up		
Foam roller	See Appendix A	
Treadmill incline walk	10 mins	With backpack (10 lb), Incline 15, moderate pace
Series One: Repeat the series four times		
1. Squat with diagonal press	10/side	Moderate weight
2. Single leg lunges	15/side	Moderate weight
3. Stairs	2 mins	
Series Two: Repeat the series four times		
1. Salamanders	15/side	
2. Skipping/jump rope	1 min	
3. Burpees	10	
Series Three: Repeat the series three times		
1. Oblique crunch off ball	12/side	
2. Pull/press	12/side	Light to moderate weight
3. Lawnmower	15/side	Moderate weight

SERIES ONE
(Repeat the series four times)

1. SQUAT WITH DIAGONAL
PRESS (OPPOSITE)

Targeted Muscles: Front and back of legs, buttocks, shoulders, abdominals, upper back, front and back of arms

Stand with your feet shoulder-width apart. Hold a single dumbbell with both hands and bend your hips and knees into a squat position (see Squats, page 119). Keep your knees behind your toes and your chest up. Push through your heels and stand up, rotating to the left and pressing the weight upward at a 45° angle while turning the hips and lifting the right heel up off the floor. Return to centre, going immediately back into a squat position, then complete the same movement pattern, this time rotating to the right. Alternate between the right and left sides for a total of 10 repetitions per side.

2. SINGLE LEG LUNGES (LEFT)

Targeted Muscles: Front and back of legs, buttocks, abdominals

Holding a dumbbell in each hand, arms at your sides, step back with one leg and place the top of your foot on an elevated and stable surface (a bench, chair, stair). Take a large step forward with your other leg. Bend your front knee until your thigh is parallel to the floor, and then stand back up by pushing through the heel of your balancing/front foot. Keep your knee tracking over your ankle rather than over your front toe. Complete 15 repetitions, then repeat with the other leg.

3. STAIRS

Targeted Muscles: Front and back of legs, buttocks, calves, your heart

Jog or run up and down a flight of stairs. Maintain your fastest pace, without stopping, for 2 minutes.

SERIES TWO
(Repeat the series four times)

1. SALAMANDERS

Targeted Muscles: Shoulders, abdominals, chest, side of torso

Start in a plank position off your hands (see Base Plank off Hands, page 123). With a tight core, crunch your right knee up to the outside of your right elbow, turning your head in the direction of your bending knee to enhance the crunch. Step the leg back, then repeat the crunch with your left knee to your left elbow. Complete this alternating movement for 15 repetitions on each side.

2. SKIPPING/JUMP ROPE (LEFT)

Targeted Muscles: Shoulders, abdominals, legs, calves, your heart

Skip or jump in place with both feet at the same time. This can be performed with a skipping/jump rope, or you can mimic the rope turning motion with your hands (to keep the arms engaged) if you do not have a rope or enough room to use a rope. Skip as quickly as you can for 1 minute.

3. BURPEES (OPPOSITE)

Targeted Muscles: Front and back of legs, upper back, shoulders, abdominals, chest, your heart

Place your hands on the floor. Jump both feet back simultaneously into a plank position, then jump both feet back up simultaneously to a deep squat position. Stand up and jump. This is one repetition. Complete 10 repetitions.

SERIES THREE
(Repeat the series three times)

1. OBLIQUE CRUNCH OFF BALL (LEFT)
Targeted Muscles: Side of torso
Place your hip on the side of an exercise ball and your feet against a solid surface, your bottom foot forward. Cross your arms over your chest, and slowly crunch upward, pushing your hip into the ball and reaching your elbow sideways, tracking over the side of your torso. Your shoulder, hip and feet should remain in a straight line, even when you are crunching upward. Complete 12 repetitions on one side, then repeat for 12 on the other side.

2. PULL/PRESS (OPPOSITE)
Targeted Muscles: Front and back of shoulders, front and back of arms, side of torso, upper back, mid-back
Start in an offset stance: right leg forward, your right hand resting on your right knee and your left hand holding a dumbbell. Pull the dumbbell up toward the side of your rib cage, then rotate through your torso (without straightening your right knee or sliding your right hand upward) and press the dumbbell directly over your shoulder so you form a T with your arms. Pause, then lower the weight back down. Complete 12 repetitions on the left and then 12 on the right side.

3. LAWNMOWER

Targeted Muscles: Front, back and inner legs, front and back of arms, front and back of shoulders, buttocks, mid-back, side of torso

From standing, and with a dumbbell on the floor in front of you, take a large step to one side so that your feet are wider than shoulder-width apart. Keep your toes pointing forward. Leaning to your right side, slowly bend at your right hip, pushing your body weight back onto your heel while you bend the right knee. Keep your left leg straight (See Stationary Side Lunge position, page 129). Rest your right elbow on your bent right knee. With the left hand, grab the dumbbell and hold it beneath you. From here, pull the weight upward in the direction of your rib cage and rotate your torso (mimicking the motion of pulling a lawnmower cord). Be sure your head turns in the same direction as your arm to protect your neck from kinking. Each pull is one repetition. Complete 15 repetitions on the right side (with left arm pulling), then switch and repeat with your left leg (right arm pulling).

KITENGE
Advanced Workout Three

Warm-up		
Foam roller and dynamic	See Appendix A	
Treadmill incline walk	10 mins	With backpack (10 lb), Incline 15, moderate pace
Series One: Repeat the series four times		
1. Squat with double press	15	Moderate weight
2. Back lunge with forward kick	12/side	Moderate weight
3. Glute bridge	1 min	Moderate weight
Series Two: Repeat the series four times		
1. Push-ups off elevated surface	10	
2. V-Press	12	Moderate weight
3. Single leg lateral raises	12	Light to moderate weight
Series Three: Repeat the series three times		
1. Side plank off feet	45 secs/side	
2. Sliding towel pike	15	
3. Plank off ball	45 secs	

SERIES ONE
(Repeat the series four times)

1. SQUAT WITH DOUBLE PRESS

Targeted Muscles: Front and back of legs, buttocks, shoulders, abdominals

Stand with your feet shoulder-width apart. Holding a dumbbell in each hand, lift each weight up so that they are parallel to the floor and the ends are in line with the front of your shoulders. Bend at your hips and knees into a squat position (see Squats, page 119). Keep your knees behind your toes and your chest up. As you push through your heels to stand back up, slowly and simultaneously push the dumbbells upward over your head. Bring them back down to the front of your shoulders. Complete 15 repetitions.

2. BACK LUNGE WITH FORWARD KICK

Targeted Muscles: Front and back of legs, calves, buttocks

Holding a dumbbell in each hand, arms at your sides, take a large step backward into a lunge. Your back knee should be just an inch off the floor, and your front knee should track nicely over the top of your ankle. Stand up out of the lunge by pushing through your front heel. Swing your back leg forward into a kick, then step back into the lunge.

Challenge your balance by not touching the ground during this transition. Complete the 12 repetitions with one leg, and then repeat with the other leg.

3. GLUTE BRIDGE

Targeted Muscles: Buttocks, back of legs

Lie on the floor with your knees bent directly over your ankles, and with feet hip-width apart. Place a dumbbell directly over the crease of your hips and hold it in place with your hands to prevent it from rolling as you perform the exercise. Squeeze your glutes and slowly lift your hips off the floor high enough to enhance the tension in your glutes, without arching your lower back. Do not allow your knees to roll inward. Most of the pressure should be in the heels of your feet as you hold this position for 1 minute.

SERIES TWO
(Repeat the series four times)

1. PUSH-UPS OFF ELEVATED SURFACE
Targeted Muscles: Abdominals, upper back, chest, shoulders

Place your toes on an elevated, stable surface (bench, chair, stair). Place your hands on the floor directly underneath your shoulders. With a tight core (as if you were slightly tucking your buttocks underneath you), slowly lower your body down in a straight line, moving your shoulders and hips at the same rate. Your chest should fall between your hands. Go as low as you can without resting your body on the floor, pause, and then push yourself up to the starting position. Complete 10 repetitions.

2. V-PRESS

Targeted Muscles: Shoulders, abdominals

Stand with your feet shoulder-width apart and your knees slightly bent. Lift the dumbbells to shoulder height, palms facing forward, so both your arms start at your sides, forming an angle slightly less than 90° at your elbows. Slowly and simultaneously push the dumbbells upward over your head in a V-formation, then lower your arms down to shoulder height. Complete 12 repetitions.

3. SINGLE LEG LATERAL RAISES

Targeted Muscles: Side of shoulders, front and back of legs, abdominals, upper back, buttocks, calves

With a dumbbell in each hand and tall posture, balance on one foot with your other leg at 90° in front of you. Slowly raise both arms up to your sides, no higher than shoulder height. Keep your shoulder blades down your back. (You know you are in the correct position if you start the exercise by lifting your shoulders up, back and down. This is called the shoulder set position.) Pause with the dumbbells at your sides for 1 second before slowly lowering the weights down. Complete 12 repetitions on one side, and then repeat on the other leg.

SERIES THREE
(Repeat the series three times)

1. SIDE PLANK OFF FEET
Targeted Muscles: Side of torso, upper back, shoulders

Lie on your side and extend your legs outward. Your feet, hips and shoulders should be in a straight line. Place your bottom elbow directly underneath your shoulder. Keep your bottom hand on the floor, perpendicular to your body. Using your oblique muscles (the sides of your torso) and a little pressure from your balancing elbow and the side of your foot, slowly raise your body weight up and lift your hips off the floor. Extend your top arm straight up so that your shoulders are in line, forming a T position with your body. Hold this position for 45 seconds, then repeat on the other side.

2. SLIDING TOWEL PIKE

Targeted Muscles: Shoulders, abdominals, front and back of legs

On a smooth surface, place a small towel underneath your toes and then take a plank position off your hands (see Base Plank off Hands, page 123). Slowly slide both of your feet toward your hands by lifting your hips up into a pike position and pulling your abdominal muscles in toward your spine. Keep your legs as straight as you can as you slide them inward. Pause when you reach the point where your body cannot go any further, then slowly slide your feet back to the starting plank position. Complete 15 repetitions.

3. PLANK OFF BALL

Targeted Muscles: Upper back, shoulders, abdominals

Place both elbows directly underneath your shoulders onto an exercise ball. Extend one leg out at a time to form a plank position. With a tight core (tilt your tailbone toward the floor), hold this position for 45 seconds.

SHUKA
Advanced Workout Four

Warm-up		
Foam roller and dynamic	See Appendix A	
Treadmill incline walk	10 mins	With backpack (12 lb), Incline 15, moderate pace
Series One: Repeat the series six times		
1. Jump squats	15	
2. Double stairs	1 min	
3. Calf raises	20/direction	Moderate weight
4. Walkouts	10	
5. Alternating jump lunges	10/side	
Series Two: Repeat the series once		
1. Treadmill incline walk	20 mins	Incline 15, fast pace (no backpack)
Series Three: Repeat the series eight times		
1. Lateral shuffles	30 secs/side	Incline 6, moderate pace

SERIES ONE
(Repeat the series six times)

1. JUMP SQUATS (LEFT)
Targeted Muscles: Front and back of legs, buttocks, abdominals, your heart

Start in a base squat position (see Squats, page 119). Bend down into a squat (keeping your knees over your ankles and your chest up) and leap from this position up off the floor, catching yourself in another squat as you come down. Complete 15 repetitions.

2. DOUBLE STAIRS
Targeted Muscles: Front and back of legs, buttocks, calves, your heart

Jog or run up a flight of stairs, taking them two stairs at a time (double). On the way down, take the stairs one stair at a time for safety. Maintain your fastest pace, without stopping, for one minute.

3. CALF RAISES (OPPOSITE)
Targeted Muscles: Calves, muscles of the feet, front of lower leg

Note that this is an exercise in three parts. Stand with your torso upright, holding a dumbbell in each hand, arms by your sides. With your toes pointing forward (targeting all aspects of the calves), raise your heels off the floor, contracting the muscles in your calves as you stand on your toes. Hold for 1–2 seconds at the top, then lower your feet back down. Complete 20 repetitions, then switch your foot position so that your toes point slightly inward (targeting the outer portion of your calves). Complete the 20 repetitions again and then switch your foot position once more, this time pointing your toes slightly outward (targeting the inner portion of your calves). Complete 20 repetitions one last time.

4. WALKOUTS

Targeted Muscles: Shoulders, abdominals, chest, upper back

Start in a standing position. Bend at the waist and place your hands on the floor (if necessary, bend your knees slightly). Once your hands are on the floor, slowly walk one hand out at a time until your back is parallel to the floor (a plank position, with your hands located directly under your shoulders). Pause, then walk one hand at a time back toward your feet. Once you reach your feet, stand up. Complete 10 repetitions.

5. ALTERNATING JUMP LUNGES (OPPOSITE)

Targeted Muscles: Front and back of legs, buttocks, abdominals

Start from standing with your hands on your hips. Take one large step forward, bending both your knees at 90° to form a lunge. From this position, jump vertically and switch your legs while in the air so you land in another lunge with the opposite leg position. Each jump is considered one repetition. Complete 20 jumps (10 per side).

SERIES TWO
(Repeat the series once)

1. TREADMILL INCLINE WALK (RIGHT)

Target muscles: Front and back of legs, buttocks, calves, your heart

Walk on a treadmill at an incline of 15 (or outside if a treadmill is not available), keeping a fast pace. The main objective is to increase your heart rate and maintain a continuous pace that will help build your muscular and cardiovascular endurance. Keep a pace that would allow you to carry on a conversation with someone while still needing to periodically catch your breath. Walk for 20 minutes.

SERIES THREE
(Repeat the series eight times)

1. LATERAL SHUFFLES

Targeted Muscles: Sides of legs, buttocks, calves, your heart

You will need a long space like a hallway to perform this exercise, as you will be covering a little distance with each step to the side. From a standing position, take a lateral (sideways) step to the right with your right foot. Carry your left foot in to the spot where your right foot was. While pushing off with the left foot, take another lateral step with your right foot. Continue this pattern for 30 seconds in the same direction, then repeat in the opposite direction (pushing off the opposite foot) for another 30 seconds. Think of this exercise as running sideways!

Note: This exercise can also be performed on a treadmill. To increase the intensity, set the treadmill at an incline of 6. For safety, keep one hand on the treadmill handle and perform at a slow speed.

MBEGE
Advanced Workout Five

Warm-up		
Foam roller	See Appendix A	
Treadmill incline walk	10 mins	With backpack (12 lb), Incline 15, moderate pace
Series One: Repeat the series four times		
1. Walking lunges	1 min	Weighted pack (12 lb)
2. Goblet squat with press-outs	15	Moderate weight
3. Standing palms-in dumbbell press	15	Moderate weight
4. Plank off ball with press-outs	1 min	
Series Two: Repeat the series four times		
1. High knees	30 secs	
2. Jumping-jack planks	50	
3. Skaters	20/side	
Series Three: Repeat the series three times		
1. 3-point mid row	12/side	Moderate to heavy weight
2. Rear delt flys	12	Light to moderate weight
3. Lawnmower	12/side	Moderate to heavy weight
4. Supermans	15	

SERIES ONE
(Repeat the series four times)

1. WALKING LUNGES (OPPOSITE)
Targeted Muscles: Front, back and inner legs, buttocks, calves

Wearing your weighted Kilimanjaro backpack, take one large step forward so that when you bend your knees they form two 90° angles. Keep your chest up during the entire exercise. Take another step forward and bend your knees once again to form two 90° angles. As you stand up from each lunge, be sure to push through your front heel to keep your front knee over your front ankle. Continue to perform walking lunges for 1 minute.

2. GOBLET SQUAT WITH PRESS-OUTS (OPPOSITE ABOVE)

Targeted Muscles: Front and back of legs, buttocks, shoulders, upper back, abdominals

Holding a dumbbell at one end with both hands (as if you were holding a large goblet), stand with your feet shoulder-width apart (see Goblet Squats, page 142). Maintain a straight back by keeping your chest up as you bend at your hips and knees, lowering into a squat position. While moving into the squat, simultaneously push the dumbbell directly outward from your chest (maintaining a slight bend in your elbows at the end of the press-out). Stand back up, bringing the dumbbell back to your chest. Complete 15 repetitions.

3. STANDING PALMS-IN DUMBBELL PRESS (OPPOSITE BELOW)

Targeted Muscles: Shoulders, abdominals

Stand with your feet shoulder-width apart and your knees slightly bent. Holding a dumbbell in each hand, lift the weights to shoulder height, keeping your palms facing in toward each other. Slowly and simultaneously push the dumbbells upward until your arms are fully extended over your shoulders, then lower your arms back down to your starting position. Complete 15 repetitions.

4. PLANK OFF BALL WITH PRESS-OUTS

Targeted Muscles: Upper back, shoulders, abdominals

Place both of your elbows directly underneath your shoulders onto an exercise ball. Extend one leg out at a time to form a plank position. With a tight core (tilt your tailbone toward the floor), slowly push the ball forward and back 2–3 inches underneath your body weight. Keep your body as still as possible as you move your arms. Continue this motion back and forth for 1 minute.

SERIES TWO
(Repeat the series four times)

1. HIGH KNEES
Targeted Muscles: Front and back of legs, abdominals, calves, your heart

Hold your hands out in front of you at waist height, palms facing the floor. Quickly jump one leg up at a time, high enough to hit your hand with your knee. Keep your chest up high during the entire movement. Repeat as quickly as you can for 30 seconds.

2. JUMPING-JACK PLANKS

Targeted Muscles: Shoulders, abdominals, upper back, your heart

From a plank position off your hands (see Base Plank off Hands, page 123), quickly jump both feet simultaneously outward to shoulder-width apart, then back to centre. Complete 50 repetitions as quickly as you can.

3. SKATERS (OPPOSITE)

Targeted Muscles: Buttocks, front and back of legs, calves, muscles of the feet, your heart

Start with your knees slightly bent and your hips slightly pushed backward. Leap from your left foot as far to the right side as you can, landing on the right foot in the slightly bent-over position you started in. Repeat this leap in the other direction. Complete 20 repetitions on each side. Tip: Placing a flat, non-slip surface (e.g. a yoga mat) on the floor beside you can help you to gauge distance.

SERIES THREE
(Repeat the series three times)

1. 3-POINT MID ROW (RIGHT)

Targeted Muscles: Front and back of arms, front and back of shoulders, mid-back, upper back

Holding a dumbbell in your right hand, rest your left hand on a platform, such as an exercise bench or a chair, for support. Keeping your back straight and your shoulders parallel to the floor, slowly pull the weight up toward the outside of your rib cage. Lower the weight down to your starting position. Complete 12 repetitions per side.

2. REAR DELT FLYS

Targeted Muscles: Upper back, back of shoulders

Holding a dumbbell in each hand, arms at your sides and palms facing thighs, bend at the hips and slightly in the knees, maintaining a straight/flat back. Slowly raise your arms out up your sides to shoulder height, with your elbows slightly bent. It is important that you can see the weights in your peripheral vision so you know you are not raising them too far behind you. Pause at shoulder height for 1 second, and then lower both arms back down below your chest. Complete 12 repetitions.

3. LAWNMOWER

Targeted Muscles: Front, back and inner legs, front and back of arms, front and back of shoulders, buttocks, mid-back, side of torso

From standing, and with a dumbbell on the floor in front of you, take a large step to one side so that your feet are wider than shoulder-width apart. Keep your toes pointing forward. Leaning to your right side, slowly bend at your right hip, pushing your body weight back onto your heel while you bend the right knee. Keep your left leg straight (See Stationary Side Lunge position, page 129). Rest your right elbow on your bent right knee. With the left hand, grab the dumbbell and hold it beneath you. From here, pull the weight upward in the direction of your rib cage and rotate your torso (mimicking the motion of pulling a lawnmower cord). Be sure your head turns in the same direction as your arm to protect your neck from kinking. Each pull is one repetition. Complete 12 repetitions on the right side (with left arm pulling), then switch and repeat with your left leg (right arm pulling)

4. SUPERMANS

Targeted Muscles: Lower back, buttocks

Lie face down on the floor with your arms fully extended above your head. Simultaneously raise your arms, legs and chest off the floor and hold for 1–2 seconds. Squeeze your lower back and buttocks at the top of the movement. Slowly lower your arms, legs and chest back to the starting position. Complete 15 repetitions.

CHAPATI
Advanced Workout Six

Warm-up		
Foam roller	See Appendix A	
Treadmill incline walk	10 mins	With backpack (12 lb), Incline 15, moderate pace
Series One: Repeat the series four times		
1. Transition lunges	45 secs/side	Moderate weight
2. Lateral lunges (dynamic)	15/side	Moderate weight
3. Step-ups	15/side	Backpack (12 lb)
Series Two: Repeat the series four times		
1. Alternating bench press	1 min	Moderate weight
2. Push-ups with alternating rotations	8/side	
Series Three: Repeat the series three times		
1. Kneeling single arm shoulder press	12/side	Moderate weight
2. Lateral single foot hops	25/side	
3. Single leg Romanian deadlifts	12/side	Moderate weight

SERIES ONE
(Repeat the series four times)

1. TRANSITION LUNGES

Targeted Muscles: Front and back of legs, buttocks, calves, your heart

Holding a dumbbell in each hand, arms at your sides, take a large step forward into a lunge position with your right leg, remembering to keep your knee tracking over your ankle. Push off your front (right) heel and transition into a back lunge. Repeat this process – front lunge, into back lunge, into front lunge, and so on – for 45 seconds, then repeat with the left leg.

2. LATERAL LUNGES – DYNAMIC

Targeted Muscles: Front, back and inner legs, calves, buttocks, abdominals, upper back, shoulders

Holding a dumbbell at one end with both hands, take a large step to one side so that your feet are wider than shoulder-width apart. Keep your toes pointing forward. On one side, slowly bend at the hip and push your body weight back onto your heel while you bend your knee, keeping your other leg straight. Then, push yourself back up into a standing position (using the bent leg) so that your feet meet back in the middle. Keep the dumbbell close to your chest during the entire movement. Complete 15 repetitions on one side, then switch to the other side.

3. STEP-UPS

Targeted Muscles: Front and back of legs, buttocks, calves

Wearing your weighted Kilimanjaro backpack, stand up straight, facing direct to a solid platform (the higher the platform, the more advanced the exercise). The first stair of a staircase is a great beginner height. An exercise bench is a great height for the intermediate and advanced. Step on the platform by extending your right leg and pushing through the right heel. Bring your left foot up to meet your right, then step down with your left foot. Repeat the movement pattern for 15 repetitions, then switch, placing the left foot on the platform and completing another 15 repetitions.

SERIES TWO
(Repeat the series four times)

1. ALTERNATING BENCH PRESS
Targeted Muscles: Front and backs of arms, shoulders, chest

With a dumbbell in each hand, lie on your back with your knees bent and feet flat on the floor. Start with arms extended, both weights above your chest, palms facing forward. Slowly lower your right arm, maintaining a 90° angle (your wrist should track over your elbow). Lower your arm as far as possible without resting your elbow on the floor. Pause at the bottom for 1 second, then press the weight back up to the starting position. Perform the same movement with the left arm. Continue the alternating pattern for 1 minute.

2. PUSH-UPS WITH ALTERNATING
ROTATIONS (OPPOSITE)

Targeted Muscles: Abdominals, upper back, chest, shoulders

Start in a plank position off your toes with your hands directly underneath your shoulders. With a tight core (as if you were slightly tucking your buttocks underneath you), slowly lower your body down in a straight line, moving your shoulders and hips at the same rate. Your chest should fall between your hands. Go as low as you can without resting your body on the floor, pause, and then push yourself back up to the starting position. Once you reach the plank position, slowly raise your right hand off the floor and, maintaining a straight arm, rotate your torso until your arm is vertical, your body forming a T with your balancing arm. Slowly rotate down to the plank position and repeat the push-up with rotation on the other arm. Each push-up with one rotation is a repetition on that side. Complete 8 repetitions per side.

SERIES THREE
(Repeat the series three times)

1. KNEELING SINGLE ARM
SHOULDER PRESS (RIGHT)

Targeted Muscles: Shoulders, abdominals, side of torso, buttocks

Kneel on your right knee and hold a dumbbell in your right hand with your arm at 90°. From this position, slowly press the dumbbell up, and then lower your arm back down to 90°, Maintain an upright position with your torso. Complete 12 repetitions on the right side, then repeat on the left knee, with the left arm.

2. LATERAL SINGLE FOOT HOPS

Targeted Muscles: Buttocks, front of legs, calves, muscles of the feet

Stand on one foot and jump laterally (to the side) as far as you can without losing your balance. Pause, and then jump again in the same direction (you might need to flip around if you run out of space). Complete 25 repetitions per side, then repeat on the other foot.

1

3. SINGLE LEG ROMANIAN DEADLIFTS

Targeted Muscles: Upper back, front and back of legs, buttocks, calves

Holding a dumbbell in each hand in front of your thighs, palms facing each other, stand with your feet shoulder-width apart. Lift one leg back and upward as you simultaneously drop your torso forward. Keep your arms straight and guide the weights as closely down the front of your balancing leg as possible to protect your back. Maintain a straight (flat) back during the entire movement, and keep your shoulders back so they do not roll forward. When you feel a stretch in the back of your balancing leg, pause, and then hinge back up to your starting position while keeping most of your body weight in your heel. Keep your hips as level as possible throughout the movement. Complete 12 repetitions, then switch to the other leg.

2

3

UGALI
Advanced Workout Seven

Warm-up		
Foam roller	See Appendix A	
Treadmill incline walk	10 mins	With backpack (12 lb), Incline 15, moderate pace
Series One: Repeat the series four times		
1. Walking lunges	1 min	Weighted pack (15 lb)
2. Back lunge with hop	15/side	Moderate weight
3. Lateral step-ups	20/side	
Series Two: Repeat the series four times		
1. Single leg goblet squats	15/side	Moderate weight
2. Single leg glute bridge pulses	20/side	
3. Long jumps	20	
Series Three: Repeat the series three times		
1. Mountain climbers	30 secs	
2. Side plank with leg lifts	30 secs/side	
3. Plank with alternating shoulder taps	15/side	
4. Skipping/jump rope	1 min	

SERIES ONE
(Repeat the series four times)

1. WALKING LUNGES (OPPOSITE)
Targeted Muscles: Front, back and inner legs, buttocks, calves

Wearing your weighted Kilimanjaro backpack, take one large step forward so that when you bend your knees they form two 90° angles. Keep your chest up during the entire exercise. Take another step forward and bend your knees once again to form two 90° angles. As you stand up from each lunge, be sure to push through your front heel to keep your front knee over your front ankle. Continue to perform walking lunges for 1 minute.

2. BACK LUNGE WITH HOP (OPPOSITE)

Targeted Muscles: Front and back of legs, calves, buttocks

Holding a dumbbell in each hand, arms at your sides, take a large step backward into a lunge. Your back knee should be just an inch off the floor, and your front knee should track nicely over your ankle. Stand back up out of the lunge by pushing through your front heel. Swing your back leg forward and tuck your knee in toward your body, then hop on the balancing foot. Challenge your balance by jumping as high as you can and by not touching the ground during this transition. Complete 15 repetitions with one leg, and then repeat with the other leg.

3. LATERAL STEP-UPS (ABOVE)

Targeted Muscles: Front and back of legs, buttocks, calves

Stand up straight, facing sideways to an elevated platform. (The higher the platform, the more advanced the exercise. The first stair of a staircase is a great beginner height. An exercise bench is a great height for the intermediate and advanced.) Step on the platform by extending the hip and the knee of your right leg, and place your foot fully on the platform down with your toes facing forward. Place most of your pressure in the middle of your right foot as you step up and bring your left foot to meet your right. Step down with the left leg, then the right, to retake your starting position. Complete 20 repetitions, then turn around complete 20 repetitions leading with the left leg.

SERIES TWO
(Repeat the series three times)

1. SINGLE LEG GOBLET SQUATS (OPPOSITE)
Targeted Muscles: Front and back of legs, buttocks
Hold a dumbbell at one end with both hands (as if you were holding a large goblet). Sit on a bench and position your feet so that your knees are bent at 90° angles. Feet in place, stand back up. Raise one foot off the floor, then bend at your hips and knee, lowering down to a seated position. Keeping your leg raised and your chest up, slowly come back to standing, pushing through your heel. Hold the dumbbell close to your chest and keep your knee over your ankle (you should be able to see your toe) throughout the entire movement. Complete 15 repetitions with one leg, then switch legs and repeat.

2. SINGLE LEG GLUTE BRIDGE
PULSES (RIGHT)
Targeted Muscles: Buttocks, back of legs
Lie on the floor with your knees bent directly over your ankles, and with feet hip-width apart. Raise one leg off the ground. Squeeze your glutes and slowly lift your hips off the floor, high enough to enhance the tension in your glutes without arching your lower back. Do not allow the knee of your supporting leg to roll inward. Most of the pressure should be in the heel of your foot as you hold this position for 1–2 seconds at the top. Lower your hips without resting them on the floor. Remember to squeeze your glutes before lifting your hips upward for each pulse. Complete 20 pulses, and then repeat with the other leg.

1   2   3

3. LONG JUMPS (ABOVE)

Targeted Muscles: Front and back of legs, buttocks, abdominals, calves, your heart

Stand with your feet shoulder-width apart. Bend at the knees and the hips, and swing your arms as far back as you can. Use your momentum to take a giant leap forward. Try to land on the heels of your feet, and stick each landing. Complete 20 repetitions.

SERIES THREE
(Repeat the series three times)

1. MOUNTAIN CLIMBERS (OPPOSITE)

Targeted Muscles: Shoulders, front and back of arms, chest, abdominals, hip flexors, front and back of legs, your heart

Start in a plank position off your hands (see Base Plank off Hands, page 123). With a tight core, jump your right knee up toward your chest, landing on the ball of your foot. Jump again, pushing the right leg back while simultaneously bringing the left knee up toward your chest, landing on the ball of your left foot. Both your feet should land at the same time. Making sure to maintain good form, complete this alternating movement as quickly as possible for 30 seconds.

2. SIDE PLANK WITH LEG LIFTS

Targeted Muscles: Side of torso, buttocks, shoulders, abdominals, upper back

Lie on your side and extend your legs outward. Your feet, hips and shoulders should be in a straight line. Place your bottom elbow directly underneath your shoulder. Keep your bottom hand on the floor, perpendicular to your body. Using your oblique muscles (the sides of your torso) and a little pressure from your balancing elbow and the side of your foot, slowly raise your body weight up and lift your hips off the floor. Extend your top arm straight up so that your shoulders are in line, forming a T position with your body. From here, slowly raise your top leg up as high as your body will allow, and then lower without rotating or compromising the lift of your torso. Repeat this motion for 30 seconds on one side, then switch and repeat on the other side.

3. PLANK WITH ALTERNATING
SHOULDER TAPS

Targeted Muscles: Shoulders, abdominals, upper back

From a plank position off your hands (see Base Plank off Hands, page 123), lift your right hand off the floor and tap your left shoulder. Place your right hand down. Lift your left hand off the floor and tap your right shoulder. Continue this alternating pattern for 15 repetitions on each side. Keep your hips as still as possible to get the most out of this exercise.

4. SKIPPING/JUMP ROPE

Targeted Muscles: Shoulders, abdominals, legs, calves, your heart

Skip or jump in place with both feet at the same time. This can be performed with a skipping/jump rope, or you can mimic the rope turning motion with your hands (to keep the arms engaged) if you do not have a rope or enough room to use a rope. Skip as quickly as you can for 1 minute.

ACACIA
Advanced Workout Eight

Warm-up		
Foam roller and dynamic	See Appendix A	
Treadmill incline walk	10 mins	With backpack (20 lb), Incline 15, moderate pace
Series One: Repeat the series four times		
1. Double stairs	1 min	
2. Burpees	10	
3. Single stairs	1 min	
4. Wide-narrow jump squats	15 each	
5. Double stairs	1 min	
6. Long jumps	20	
7. Single stairs	1 min	
8. Side-to-side jump lunges	15/side	
Series Two: Repeat the series once		
1. Treadmill incline walk	20 mins	Incline 15, fast pace
Series Three: Repeat the series eight times		
1. Lateral shuffles	30 secs/side	Incline 6, moderate pace

SERIES ONE
(Repeat the series four times)

1. DOUBLE STAIRS

Targeted Muscles: Front and back of legs, buttocks, calves, your heart

Jog or run up a flight of stairs, taking them two stairs at a time (double). On the way down, take the stairs one stair at a time for safety. Maintain your fastest pace, without stopping, for 1 minute.

2. BURPEES (ABOVE)

Targeted Muscles: Front and back of legs, upper back, shoulders, abdominals, chest, your heart

Place your hands on the floor. Jump both feet back simultaneously into a plank position, then jump both feet back up simultaneously to a deep squat position. Stand up and jump. This is one repetition. Complete 10 repetitions.

3. SINGLE STAIRS

Targeted Muscles: Front and back of legs, buttocks, calves, your heart

Jog or run up and down a flight of stairs (one stair at a time). Maintain your fastest pace, without stopping, for 1 minute.

4. WIDE–NARROW JUMP SQUATS

Targeted Muscles: Front, back and inner legs, buttocks, calves, your heart

Start in a wide squat position (see Squats, page 119), with feet farther than shoulder-width apart. From the squat, jump up into a narrow squat position, with both feet together. From the narrow squat position, jump back into a wide squat position. If you have knee problems, do not go past parallel. Keep your knees over your ankles (you should be able to see your toes throughout the entire movement). Keep your chest up during the entire movement. Repeat as quickly as you can for 15 repetitions of each.

5. DOUBLE STAIRS

Targeted Muscles: Front and back of legs, buttocks, calves, your heart

Jog or run up a flight of stairs, taking them two stairs at a time (double). On the way down, take the stairs one stair at a time for safety. Maintain your fastest pace, without stopping, for 1 minute.

6. LONG JUMPS (ABOVE)

Targeted Muscles: Front and back of legs, buttocks, abdominals, calves, your heart

Stand with your feet shoulder-width apart. Bend at the knees and the hips, and swing your arms as far back as you can. Use your momentum to take a giant leap forward. Try to land on the heels of your feet, and stick each landing. Complete 20 repetitions.

7. SINGLE STAIRS

Targeted Muscles: Front and back of legs, buttocks, calves, your heart

Jog or run up and down a flight of stairs (one stair at a time). Maintain your fastest pace, without stopping, for 1 minute.

8. SIDE-TO-SIDE JUMP LUNGES (BELOW)

Targeted Muscles: Front, back and inner legs, buttocks, abdominals, your heart

From a standing position, take a large step to one side so that your feet are wider than shoulder-width apart. Keep your toes pointing forward. Slowly bend at the hip and push your body weight back onto your heel while you bend one knee. Keep your other leg straight. Pushing from your bent leg, jump yourself back up to centre and land in another side lunge on the opposite leg. Complete 15 repetitions per side.

SERIES TWO
(Repeat the series four times)

1. TREADMILL INCLINE WALK
(SEE PAGE 245)

Target muscles: Front and back of legs, buttocks, calves, your heart

Walk on a treadmill at an incline of 15 (or outside if a treadmill is not available), keeping a fast pace. The main objective is to increase your heart rate and maintain a continuous pace that will help build your muscular and cardiovascular endurance. Keep a pace that would allow you to carry on a conversation with someone while still needing to periodically catch your breath. Walk for 20 minutes.

SERIES THREE

(Repeat the series eight times)

1. LATERAL SHUFFLES

Targeted Muscles: Sides of legs, buttocks, calves, your heart

You will need a long space like a hallway to perform this exercise, as you will be covering a little distance with each step to the side. From a standing position, take a lateral (sideways) step to the right with your right foot. Carry your left foot in to the spot where your right foot was. While pushing off with the left foot, take another lateral step with your right foot. Continue this pattern for 30 seconds in the same direction, then repeat in the opposite direction (pushing off the opposite foot) for another 30 seconds. Think of this exercise as running sideways!

Note: This exercise can also be performed on a treadmill. To increase the intensity, set the treadmill at an incline of 6. For safety, keep one hand on the treadmill handle and perform at a slow speed.

Appendix A

FOAM ROLLER WARM-UP

1. QUADRICEPS (LEFT)
(Front of leg)
Lie down with the front of your thighs on top of the foam roller. Use your hands to slowly push yourself forward and back over the roller between your hip and knee joints. For a more intense pressure, lift one leg up or rest it on top of the other leg.

2. GLUTES (LEFT)
(Buttocks)
Seated squarely on the foam roller, lean to one side until only one side of your buttocks is in contact with the roller. With your hands behind you, and your feet placed on the floor, slowly roll the side of your buttocks back and forth by using a push/pull motion with your hands and feet. Repeat on the other side.

3. ILIOTIBIAL (IT) BAND (LEFT)
(Side of leg and hip)
Seated on the foam roller, lean to one side until the side of your leg (below the hip joint) is in contact with the roller. With your hand behind you, and your foot placed on the floor in front of the leg that is being rolled out, slowly roll the side of your hip and leg (the IT band) back and forth using a push/pull motion with your hand and foot.

4. GASTROCNEMIUS AND SOLEUS (RIGHT)
(Calves)

Rest the backs of your lower legs on the foam roller. Lift your body up with your hands behind you and slowly push and pull your legs (between the ankle and knee joints) with your hands. For more intense pressure, cross your legs so only one leg is resting on the foam roller at a time.

5. LATISSIMUS DORSI (BELOW)
(Back and underneath the armpit)

Lie on your side with one arm up and over the foam roller. The point of contact should be the area of your rib cage just beneath your armpit. Just holding here might be enough pressure. If you want more pressure, place one foot in front of you and use that to slowly push and pull your body weight over the foam roller, going no further than half a roll of the foam roller.

6. DELTOIDS AND LATISSIMUS DORSI (LEFT)
(Shoulders and back)

Begin by kneeling on the ground. Place your wrists on a foam roller two feet in front of you. Slowly roll the foam roller (using your wrists) away from your hips and press your chest toward the ground. You should feel this stretch in your lats and the front of your shoulders. Hold this position for 30 seconds, and then gently roll in the reverse direction out of the posture.

7. ERECTOR SPINAE (BELOW)
(Back muscles)

Begin by lying on the foam roller with it positioned on your mid-back. Cross your arms over your chest and lift your buttocks off the floor by pushing through the heels of your feet. Slowly roll the foam roller upward along your back by walking your feet outward until the roller reaches your mid-upper back. Do not roll further than your shoulders, to avoid rolling up toward your neck.

ACKNOWLEDGEMENTS

Thank you to the Rocky Mountain Books team for investing in our book. It has been a wonderful year working together, and an honour to be added to the incredible RMB author list. A special thank you to Don Gorman for seeing the potential in *Polepole*. To Meaghan Craven at Craven Editorial, a big thank-you for your incredibly quick turnaround and positive approach to the editing process.

Capturing ninety-four different exercises in three hours was no easy task. Claudine Lavoie, you pulled it off beautifully. I appreciate your time, patience and attention to detail during every photo-shoot.

I'd like to thank Kailie Fearon at Bloom Hair Studio, and Sheena Ohnysty for their hair and makeup artistry. Your talents help make every photo-shoot easier, when I'm feeling my best.

To all of my dedicated and inspiring clients - it's a genuine dream to wake up each day and be on the sidelines to watch you achieve your fitness goals, and see how it translates into your lives. I am so grateful to be a little part of it.

Thank you to my favourite mom, and favourite dad for setting an example of what work ethic is. All of your love, sacrifice and encouragement have given me the confidence to live the life I always wanted.

Thank you to Jan and Marge, my favourite brother and wonderful friends for believing in me and supporting me in everything I do.

Paul and Erinne, thank you for trusting in the process and putting your fitness programming in my hands. It was and continues to be an honour and a highlight of my week. I'm so proud of you both. Thank you for accepting my proposal to make this book together and sharing such a personal experience with honesty and grace.

To my husband Mike, I can never put into words just how much I appreciate how you love me for who I am, and support my insatiable desire to see the world and climb higher peaks. You are the kindest person I've ever known and I'm so grateful for the life we have.

—Angela

Summiting Kilimanjaro took a whole team, and all are mentioned throughout this book. Thank you to everyone who contributed to Paul's and my climb.

Thank you to the crew at RMB who continue to show enthusiasm and drive for *Polepole*. Our goal has been to help as many others as possible to also achieve a successful summit, and your work has contributed to this in a major way.

To those in the writing and publishing community who helped me both directly and indirectly with this project, thank you. Too many to name, but some who had a direct influence in particular: TM, MB, ME, DMC, AK, NS, JS, EP, BB. A huge thank you to Jannie Edwards, my first creative writing teacher. You provided me with my first writing tool-kit and continue to offer both mentorship and friendship that I am so grateful for.

I don't know if I would be so brave as to attempt to climb a mountain, or to publish a book about it, if I didn't have such a strong web of support. To my friends, siblings, in-laws, parents, and grandparents (living and departed), all my love and gratitude. Thank you for helping to hold my life together while I write. For looking after my kid (and dog). For providing space for me to work (looking at you, Caffiend!). For letting me off the hook on an overdue phone call or email.

Thank you, Angela, for allowing me to share my story alongside your expertise. Workouts with you continue to anchor my weeks, but your friendship means even more.

Finally, Paul, you've been a solid presence in my life since that first hike up a mountain in Jasper. My Kilimanjaro story is intertwined with yours. Thank you for letting me share it. And Anouk: the exuberance you've had for life since the moment you figured out how to throw your arms around in the air inspires me to push for just as much joy and excitement in my own life. Thank you.

—Erinne